The Logic of Intelligence Analysis

This book discusses the application of hypothesis testing to the practice of intelligence analysis.

By drawing on longstanding procedures of scientific method, particularly hypothesis testing, this book strongly critiques standard intelligence analytic practices. It shows these practices to be inadequate, as they are illogical in terms of what formal philosophy says any intelligence analysts can realistically be expected to know, and for the future when analysts will face pressures to adapt to digital age modeling techniques. The methodology focuses on identifying and remedying analytic errors caused by analyst cognitive biases and by foreign denial and deception. To demonstrate that it is a practical tool, it walks analysts through a case study, step by step, to show how its hypothesis testing can be implemented. It also invites a comparative test in the real world with any other intelligence methodologies to assess its strengths and weaknesses in predicting the outcome of an actual "live" intelligence issue.

This book will be of much interest to students of intelligence studies, public policy, and national security, as well as practitioners.

Karl Spielmann is a retired Senior Analyst who worked in the Denial and Deception component of the Central Intelligence Agency's Directorate of Intelligence and on the U.S. inter-agency National Intelligence Council. He holds a PhD in Political Science from Harvard University.

The Logic of Intelligence Analysis

Why Hypothesis Testing Matters

Karl Spielmann

Routledge
Taylor & Francis Group

LONDON AND NEW YORK

First published 2018 by Routledge

2 Park Square, Milton Park, Abingdon, Oxfordshire OX14 4RN

52 Vanderbilt Avenue, New York, NY 10017

Routledge is an imprint of the Taylor & Francis Group, an informa business

First issued in paperback 2020

British Library Cataloguing-in-Publication Data
A catalogue record for this book is available from the British Library

Library of Congress Cataloging-in-Publication Data
Names: Spielmann, Karl Frederick, author.
Title: The logic of intelligence analysis: why hypothesis testing
matters / Karl Spielmann.
Description: Abingdon, Oxon; New York, NY: Routledge, 2018. |
Includes bibliographical references and index.
Identifiers: LCCN 2018013812 | ISBN 9781138601963 (hardback)
| ISBN 9780429469817 (e-book)
Subjects: LCSH: Intelligence service–United States–Methodology.
| Statistical hypothesis testing. | National security–United
States–Evaluation.
Classification: LCC UB251.U5 S725 2018 | DDC 327.1273–dc23
LC record available at https://lccn.loc.gov/2018013812

ISBN: 978-1-138-60196-3 (hbk)
ISBN: 978-0-367-60694-7 (pbk)

Typeset in Times New Roman
by Wearset Ltd, Boldon, Tyne and Wear

Contents

Illustrations

Tables

Boxes

Preface
Revisiting an old problem—new concerns, new remedies

A serious reckoning is looming for intelligence analysis, at least as it has long been practiced in the United States. Its traditional way of doing things—only marginally challenged for decades—is starkly incompatible with the requirements of the digital age. Intelligence has already had to deal with a new type of threat because of advances in computer capabilities—cyber threats. The digital age has also brought new capabilities and complications for intelligence technical collection.

Can a major impact on all-source intelligence analysis, therefore, somehow be avoided? I don't think so. The basic task of intelligence analysis is prediction: to provide a heads up for policymakers on foreign developments that affect the country's interests.[1] Computerized statistical probability analysis, using ever more sophisticated mathematical modeling techniques, has already been proving its worth in all sorts of applications in the civilian world. Can intelligence analysis really steer clear of such techniques for prediction without appearing to be wedded to what will seem to many to be "horse and buggy" analysis that is arguably less credible?

But before trying to jump into the deep end of this new pool, it makes sense for intelligence analysis to make some less dramatic but still consequential changes. Moving toward approaches that broadly emulate computerized statistical probability techniques, by comparing alternative answers to a given intelligence problem, is a prudent step to take. In this handbook, I offer an approach to help analysts now and position them for the future, based on three articles that I originally published in the *International Journal of Intelligence and Counterintelligence* over the past six years.

Chapter 1 provides an update for these articles, placing them in the context of some of today's key intelligence concerns about prediction, particularly raised by Professor Philip Tetlock (and others, such as Richard Clarke, former counter terrorism advisor to President George W. Bush). Tetlock's concerns are based on his recent contract work for U.S. Intelligence and reflected in his book *Superforecasting: The Art and*

Science of Prediction.[2] However, in this handbook I draw on my previously published articles to show how one can come at the same prediction problem from a different perspective—that of an intelligence insider. My background of almost three decades in intelligence analysis, serving in a variety of positions as analyst and manager, enables me to offer some contrasting—but also complementary—solutions.

Chapter 2 presents my basic methodology, focused particularly on improving threat analysis, which argues for intelligence organizations to use comparative hypothesis testing rather than the traditional approach of relying on group consensus to predict threats and other issues. The methodology emphasizes the importance of improving methods for addressing both foreign denial and deception (D&D) and analyst cognitive biases that can distort intelligence analysis. And it provides various techniques to do so.

Chapter 3 is an illustrative case study intended as an instructional aid for working analysts. It demonstrates how the analytic techniques proposed in Chapter 2 can be applied in a step by step manner to reach sound conclusions on the likelihood of some threat (or other intelligence issue). It shows how rigorous and thorough hypothesis testing can be done to afford policymakers and military commanders transparent—that is, clear and precise—numerically based judgments, and in a timely manner, on what is a more or less likely course of action by an adversary.

Chapter 4 looks to the future challenge that digital age computerized statistical probability analysis, using sophisticated mathematical modeling techniques, poses for intelligence analysis. (The chapter's peg point for discussing the use of such techniques in the civilian world is the work of the well-known U.S. prognosticator, Nate Silver.) Based on key sources of error and other obstacles in intelligence analysis that my method addresses, the chapter offers some essential guidance for adaptations that digital age modeling needs to make to be a viable future tool for intelligence analysis.

My approach is not a novel way to get answers. I rely heavily on the breakthrough work of Richards Heuer, a former U.S. intelligence officer who devised an analysis of competing hypotheses (ACH) methodology decades ago.[3] He pioneered in bringing scientific method, as refined by the prominent thinker and philosopher of science, Sir Karl Popper, many years earlier, to intelligence analysis.[4] My method is simply a further adaptation of their hypothesis testing approaches.

Besides the fact that such approaches exist, and are rooted in longstanding procedures of scientific inquiry, what is noteworthy is that, throughout at least the almost three decades that I was in the business (and I believe still today), they have had only a marginal impact on intelligence analysis. Clearly this bodes poorly for intelligence analysis being able and willing to make the even greater adaptation that the digital age will eventually demand.

But the big questions are why such approaches calling for hypothesis testing have not had greater traction over the years and what, if anything, can be done to "sell" them more effectively? In Chapter 1, I offer some speculations, based on my intelligence background, on the first question and new—perhaps even unorthodox or idiosyncratic—remedies, based in part on my academic background, in response to the second question.

One remedy is to look to simple logic—what I call "the logic of intelligence analysis"—to give concerned intelligence analysts, managers, and other intelligence professionals more ammunition to argue in house for hypothesis testing. This remedy draws on the epistemological roots of intelligence analysis, of what analysts can reasonably be expected to know about their subject matter, to show in a logical line of argument that the traditional group consensus approach is inadequate to address probability issues for making predictions.

The other remedy—which is highly consistent with the first—is go beyond comparing hypotheses on some intelligence issues and compare different methods on the issues. Comparing different methods could include: the traditional group consensus approach; my method; Tetlock's; and any other approach (old or new) whose utility intelligence practitioners may wish to assess. The aim is to see which method comes closest to "getting it right" in making a predictive judgment on the same intelligence issue when the real world's verdict comes in—and then draw appropriate lessons from these results. In my view, in gauging the pluses and minuses of a methodology, this is the only solid way to do it. No manner of endorsements or critiques from prominent academics or intelligence professionals can be as authoritative as such comparative testing.

Notes

1 The use of prediction is not embraced by some intelligence practitioners and others as the primary function of intelligence. (For example, Eric Denece, director and founder of the French Centre of Intelligence Studies, has said flatly of intelligence organizations: "They should not try to, and are not able to, predict the future." "The Revolution in Intelligence Affairs: 1989–2003," *International Journal of Intelligence and Counterintelligence*, vol. 27, no. 1, Spring 2014, p. 39.) Indeed, prediction is by no means the sole function of intelligence, because providing accurate insights on current matters of concern is also a key mission. For example, the intelligence failure on Iraqi Weapons of Mass Destruction (WMD) was not so much a predictive failure but more a matter of misjudging the current status of Saddam's programs in the run up to the Allies' invasion (see also Chapter 1, note 11). Nevertheless, even this wound up being, in effect, a wrong prediction of what the Allies could expect to encounter once they got there (which, as bad as the failure turned out to be, at least meant that the Allies did not actually face Iraqi forces armed with WMD).

For me, the case for prediction as the primary (albeit not sole) function of intelligence can be simply made: (a) intelligence organizations are generously funded by governments to get and make use of secrets; (b) they therefore have certain unique information on adversaries that other organizations lack; and (c) as difficult and fraught with pitfalls as it may be for intelligence organizations to predict, who else could governments be expected to look to for a heads up on dangers from these adversaries?

2 See Chapter 1, note 16.

3 Heuer's ACH methodology along with his other works are readily available on the Internet. Originally developed in the 1970s, a software version of the methodology was made available in recent years, which considerably facilitates its use by analysts. Heuer presents an overview in Chapter 8 of his *Psychology of Intelligence Analysis*, Kindle ed., Center for the Study of Intelligence, Central Intelligence Agency, Washington, DC, 2016. (See also his *Structured Analytic Techniques for Intelligence Analysis* [with Randolph H. Pherson], 2nd ed., CQ Press, Los Angeles, 2014; and Neil Thomason, "Alternative Competing Hypotheses," *Field Evaluation in the Intelligence and Counterintelligence Context: Workshop Summary*, The National Academies Press, Washington, DC, 2010.)

I particularly share Heuer's appreciation of the importance of inconsistency testing and, more generally, his longstanding concern with the impact of cognitive biases on an intelligence analyst's treatment of hypotheses and evidence. However, as I point up in discussing various issues throughout the following chapters, my method is distinctive from Heuer's in several respects: (1) it includes a zero-based review of a dominant view's data support and reasoning to set the stage for an inconsistency test; (2) it follows up an inconsistency test with a missing data test to take into account other strengths (or weaknesses) of a given hypothesis; (3) it puts a greater emphasis on the importance of using many hypotheses rather than a few; (4) in connection with this, it calls to attention the significance of "shared consistency," not just inconsistency, as a key source of error; and (5) it streamlines Heuer's measures to refine inconsistency testing, based on the expectation that inconsistency determinations will be challenged by interested parties in any case—instead, my method calls for including a rebuttal process which, on particularly important issues, outside reviewers should oversee.

4 Sir Karl Popper's methodological writings are also readily available on the Internet. For an easy overview of his basic approach, see the Internet entry for "Science as Falsification" originally published in *Conjectures and Refutations*, 1963. The importance of inconsistency as an analytic tool—which is the main metric in Heuer's and my alternative analysis methodology (see Chapter 1, note 9)—is probably most famously reflected in Popper's falsification principle as a test of the validity of a scientific theory. On the colloquial level, Popper used the metaphor of the "Black Swan" to convey his approach: to test the proposition that "all swans are white," one could either try to find larger and larger samples of white swans or, more simply and rigorously, look for a black swan. It would take the discovery of only one black swan to disprove the proposition. See also, Chapter 1, note 14.

Bibliography

Clarke, Richard (with R.P. Eddy), *Warnings: Finding Cassandras to Stop Catastrophes*, Harper Collins, New York, 2017.

Denece, Eric, "The Revolution in Intelligence Affairs: 1989–2003," *International Journal of Intelligence and Counterintelligence*, vol. 27, no. 1, Spring 2014, pp. 27–41.

Heuer, Richards J., *Psychology of Intelligence Analysis*, Kindle ed., Center for the Study of Intelligence, Central Intelligence Agency, Washington, DC, 2016.

Heuer, Richards J. (with Randolph H. Pherson), *Structured Analytic Techniques for Intelligence Analysis*, 2nd ed., CQ Press, Los Angeles, 2014.

Popper, Sir Karl, "Science as Falsification," in *Conjectures and Refutations: The Growth of Scientific Knowledge*, Routledge Classics, London, 2000.

Silver, Nate, *The Signal and the Noise: Why So Many Predictions Fail—But Some Don't*, Penguin Books, New York, 2012.

Spielmann, Karl, "Strengthening Intelligence Threat Analysis," *International Journal of Intelligence and Counterintelligence*, vol. 25, no. 1, Spring 2012, pp. 19–43.

Spielmann, Karl, "Using Enhanced Analytic Techniques for Threat Analysis: A Case Study Illustration," *International Journal of Counterintelligence*, vol. 27, no. 1, Spring 2014, pp. 132–155.

Spielmann, Karl, "I Got Algorithm: Can There Be a Nate Silver in Intelligence?" *International Journal of Intelligence and Counterintelligence*, vol. 29, no. 3, Fall 2016, pp. 525–544.

Tetlock, Philip E., *Expert Political Judgment: How Good Is It? How Can We Know?* Princeton University Press, Princeton, 2005.

Tetlock, Philip E. (with Dan Gardner), *Superforecasting: The Art and Science of Prediction*, Crown Publishers, New York, 2015.

Thomason, Neil, "Alternative Competing Hypotheses," *Field Evaluation in the Intelligence and Counterintelligence Context: Workshop Summary*, The National Academies Press, Washington, DC, 2010.

those authored by former intelligence officers. In the analysts' view, these officers: actually know what it is like to task collectors for needed secrets; have experienced the rough and tumble of moving an analysis through the layers of bureaucracy; and have had to persuade (through writings or in face to face meetings) policy consumers or military commanders who must make tough—perhaps life and death—decisions based on their analysis. But, even here, significantly changing standard analytic practice has been an uphill battle—as the limited impact of Heuer's own very solid work on hypothesis testing, which was originally developed in the 1970s, attests.

Intelligence officers—or former ones, such as myself—have some special concerns and constraints in devising methods for hypothesis testing. Unlike working with similar approaches in academe, intelligence analysis has to deal with foreign denial and deception (foreign D&D, as it's known in the business) as key factors affecting accurate prediction. In short, secrets are the advantage intelligence analysts have over academics; having to cope with foreign D&D is the price these analysts pay for getting those secrets.

Having rounded out my career as the senior analyst on foreign D&D in CIA's Directorate of Intelligence, I believe that judicious treatment of the topic is essential. It is easy to either understate or overstate its impact. For example, general propaganda aside, academics who have not been in the intelligence business are less likely to have been the targets of foreign D&D. Moreover, even the bitterest of rivalries with their academic colleagues would probably not have sensitized them to the damage that can be wrought when an opponent is absolutely determined to ensure one "gets it wrong." By the same token, intelligence practitioners can sometimes become obsessive about the impact of foreign D&D (part of the cycle of overreaction and under reaction over the years—dating back to the "mole hunts" in U.S. intelligence of decades past). However, as sensible as it is to give foreign D&D serious consideration, it is not the only factor that can cause intelligence analysts to get it wrong. An analyst's own cognitive biases, for example, can be just as harmful.

The importance of dealing judiciously with foreign D&D has only increased in recent years, as controversies have bloomed about the efficacy of "hard" (or harsh) vs. "soft" vetting techniques for human sources. Another recent and growing complication is the ability of foreign adversaries to use the new technical cyber tool to deny or deceive. (In fact, cyber threats open up a whole new chapter in the history of how states from ancient times have used D&D.) In my methodology for threat analysis presented in Chapter 2, I have incorporated techniques—which would have to be regularly updated and refined by working analysts—to help cope with the serious foreign D&D challenge, particularly to double-check

1 Maybe it's time for something different

Intelligence analysis has essentially relied on a process of group consen to come up with a prediction of some threat or other foreign developm of national concern, both within individual agencies and (in the U.S.) 1 Intelligence Community (IC). Rooted in the belief that knowledgeable a seasoned veterans in the reviewing ranks of intelligence organizations a the best and most reliable quality control mechanism, this group consensi process has endured since the inception of modern U.S. Intelligence whe the Cold War got under way. Sheer inertia, maintaining bureaucratic equ ties and prerogatives, and a belief that such things as missing or over looked secrets from collectors, or poor sharing of them, are the primar culprits when big failures occur—all have contributed to keep this tradi tional process going. The net effect is that a collective mindset has been cultivated that "this is just the way intelligence analysis gets done" and there has been insufficient questioning regarding its basic soundness.

An insider's perspective on the problem

For whatever reason or combination of reasons, the traditional analytic approach hardly has been welcoming to all sorts of new ideas and approaches in the social sciences, as the decades of the Cold War and beyond have gone by.[1] The widespread assumption among its practitioners that their access to secrets made them different from academics no doubt has played an important role. Small wonder then that the latest social science breakthrough that might actually help to improve an intelligence analyst's chances of "getting it right" has usually found few takers—especially when analysts know that some new idea or approach, which might have professional appeal to them personally, simply faces them with the difficult task of then persuading their colleagues and bosses.

At least as I witnessed it, with a few exceptions, the academic writings that intelligence analysts are likely to view as offering real help are mostly the results of both human and technical vetting that the collection organizations do.

Another constraint for any methodologist seeking to provide guidance for intelligence analysts is that, for understandable security concerns, what might be possible to include in a methodology on a classified basis simply cannot be aired in a public forum. For discussion on an unclassified level, therefore, methodologists (certainly those like myself, focusing on threat issues) have to rely heavily on the next best thing: namely, post mortems on major intelligence failures that have been made public. Trying to rely on other open sources is no substitute, no matter how sophisticated the analysis. The risk of basing one's judgments on uninformed speculation about the why's and wherefore's of some threat or other major intelligence issue (especially when the impact of foreign D&D may be involved) is too high.

In devising my methodology, therefore, I have drawn heavily on the unclassified versions of two big official U.S. post mortems: those of the 9/11 attacks and the intelligence failure on Iraqi WMD. These post mortems have many useful insights on intelligence analytic practices— calling attention to both data and reasoning problems that contributed to the failures. Moreover, for a threat analysis methodology, taken together they have the virtue of covering the two basic types of threat concerns: those from terrorists and those from state adversaries. But these post mortems do not, all on their own, give the final remedies for analysis on a number of issues. That is why I view them mostly as a source of information and not as providing definitive answers and judgments that are above question.[2]

Also, these post mortems were not issued just yesterday (although the UK post mortem on Iraqi WMD—the Chilcot Committee Inquiry— emerged only in 2016). It obviously would be desirable for methodologists to be able to draw on other, more recent post mortems. But, in the larger scheme of things, the lack of more current cases can hardly be lamented. Post mortems are issued, after all, because the U.S. and other major governments judge there to have been big intelligence failures that warrant extensive after action scrutiny.

Clearly there have been many recent cases where, even if no major intelligence failures occurred or were acknowledged, considerable insights might be gleaned to refine methodologies. To name but a few: the emergence of the Arab spring and its eventual outcomes in Egypt, Libya, and Syria; the sprouting and evolution of the ISIS terrorist threat; the concerning course of Iran's nuclear program; and, perhaps above all, the nature and pace of North Korea's nuclear and long range ballistic missile programs.

Whatever internal evaluations of the effectiveness of intelligence analysis—in anticipating and tracking these threat issues—might have been conducted, methodologists working in the public domain have been afforded no reliable grist for their mills. In all of these more recent cases, however, I am convinced serious hypothesis testing could at least have helped sharpen the relevant intelligence analysts' insights.

Even if there were a larger treasure trove of publicly available material, methodologists working in the public domain would still have a hard job making a difference in how intelligence analysis is carried out. In particular, efforts to get hypothesis testing accepted as a normal practice have been no match for the staying power of group consensus as the basic way to do intelligence analysis and subject it to quality control.

In some areas, to be sure, at least some type of testing is endorsed. For example, on physical science issues, such as judging the technical feasibility of an adversary weapon achieving a certain range or accuracy, running certain tests would be accepted practice. But this does not hold true where "softer" social science issues come in—such as whether country X or leader X would mount some threat. It is here that systematically exploring various possibilities—comparing them through the use of serious hypothesis testing—makes sense. But thus far (at least unless there has been some recent breakthrough) this has not happened.

So what might help to start to turn the intelligence analysis supertanker? The best potential persuader, in my view, is ensnared in a Catch-22 but at some point might still be doable. As I later elaborate, a methodology that proved the value of hypothesis testing in some actual real world cases might make a big difference. (Historically, there has been at least a limited example of this happening.) But there would have to be some real acceptance of the methodology first by influential skeptics in order to make this possible. And then there would have to be serious follow up if hypothesis testing proved its worth in those cases. Otherwise, the opportunity to push for more widespread application would be squandered.

I believe, therefore, that concerned analysts, managers, and other intelligence professionals—sensitive to a digital age sea change looming in the future—might be able to take advantage of a new approach that simply draws on basic logic to make the case for hypothesis testing. With it, I pose a straightforward challenge for backers of maintaining the traditional group consensus approach: Can the traditional approach be justified in the face of what I call the logic of intelligence analysis that supports hypothesis testing?

Intelligence analysis, after all, is merely another branch of knowledge or field of inquiry. Formal philosophy—specifically, epistemology—can be applied to it as with any other branch of knowledge or field of inquiry.

For those engaged in intelligence analysis as a profession, knowing the roots of their field is certainly important. For example, they should be concerned about: How can we know? What can we know? When can we know it? In the logic of intelligence analysis, I lay out a sequence of assertions/ propositions (which I then summarize as seven steps in the overall argument) that lead to a basic conclusion. If readers find each of these propositions and the sequence of the argument to be sound, it is therefore logical to accept the conclusion.[3]

The logic of intelligence analysis: back to basics

Intelligence analysis has much in common with academic inquiry but is mainly known for what makes it distinctive. Its principal function is to make the most sense of what really makes intelligence special: collection from unique human and technical sources, for which governments expend a lot of resources that sustain some large bureaucracies. Collectors and all-source analysts alike share a big responsibility: to provide vital insights for policymakers on foreign developments that affect the country's interests— not only on what is currently happening in the world but, above all, on what policymakers could reasonably expect to face in at least the relatively near future.

Intelligence analysis is, therefore, shaped by its predictive mission to provide a heads up for policymakers, and by the pros (unique insights) and cons (such as risks of deception) of the special information collectors provide.[4] One side effect is that analysts' access to these secrets may tempt at least some of them to believe analytic rigor is less necessary than in academe. But if intelligence analysts are truly mindful of their power and responsibility, they should reach the opposite conclusion. Their ability to affect policy decisions, some with major life and death consequences, in fact makes analytic rigor a crucial requirement.

Besides being rigorous, however, intelligence analysis also needs to be thorough. Even a rigorous analysis will fall short, if it leaves certain essential elements of analysis out of the equation. These essential elements are pertinent for various fields of inquiry as well as intelligence analysis. A step by step approach helps identify what they are.

First, it is necessary to appreciate that analysis has two basic components: information and how one thinks about it—that is, **data** and **reasoning**. (Analysis, of course, can involve reasoning alone. But even Einstein was not content with pure theory and it would be a nonstarter for intelligence—unpersuasive to its consumers and a death sentence for its collectors.) Is there another aspect of analysis that is as basic? I don't think so.

Now let's break down these components into their essential elements.

- As for **data**, its essentials are its **quantity** and **quality** relevant to a given issue. Doesn't this cover the basics for both classified and unclassified sources?
- As for the **reasoning** applied to the data: one first wants to have **sound assumptions**; then what matters is that the deductions or inferences from these assumptions are logical. In other words, sound assumptions should be followed by a **sound logic train**. Again, is there something else as basic?

These essentials give analysts and methodologists a valuable checklist. By definition, no intelligence analysis—or methodology for intelligence analysis—can claim to be thorough if it ignores or slights any of them.

Covering all of these bases is particularly important for intelligence analysts, because they cannot make timely use of the <u>best</u> means to see if they are correct: real world **empirical verification**—routine in various scientific investigations. Intelligence analysts obviously would be greatly helped if they could run a test that would give them the real world's verdict on their proposed answer before they had to submit it to policymakers. In that event, closely probing all of the data and reasoning in the case would be much less necessary.

<u>Timing</u>, however, is the big problem in terms of intelligence analysts being able to empirically verify that their proposed answer is the **truth**. They can certainly get the real world's verdict on their proposed answer, but only when the threat (or whatever) that they predict either does or does not actually occur. This might be acceptable—even the norm—in some fields of inquiry. But it clearly fails to meet the crucial intelligence requirement of giving policymakers a needed heads up. How can intelligence analysts compensate?

When empirical verification is out of reach, the only real option open to intelligence analysts is to come up with an answer that <u>stands the best chance of being true</u>. In other words, analysts have to rely on an answer based on **probability**. To show what this entails, I take some liberties with certain philosophical distinctions and nuances to stipulate the following simple definitions: (1) I call an answer that is empirically verified—"true"; (2) I call an answer that stands the best chance of being true—or, what is the same thing, least likely to be wrong—"valid."

Despite their access to secrets, intelligence analysts, ironically, start with a handicap in trying to make valid probability judgments compared to many analysts elsewhere. Performance records underpin a wide variety of probability judgments in the civilian world. They are a sensible resource to tap, to help determine probability in some current cases, when good records are available that appropriately cover both past successes and failures. But intelligence analysts cannot tap such a resource. Intelligence performance records are generally spotty and particularly slight past successes.[5]

Thus, intelligence analysts have no choice but to try to squeeze every drop of insight out of the data and reasoning—the basic components of analysis with their essentials—available in a current case. And this, in turn, makes rigorous and thorough analysis not only important but mandatory.

But what, in fact, should analysts rigorously and thoroughly analyze to determine probability? The very definition of a valid answer makes this clear. *Given that a valid answer is supposed to stand the "best chance" of being true, an answer claiming to be valid must be compared against something. This is where the logic of intelligence analysis can really bring to light some critical considerations that tend to get overlooked. Specifically: since determining probability is the most that can be done in intelligence analysis and since this, in turn, requires some comparison to be made, the viability of any given methodology literally hinges on its ability to meet this requirement.*

In particular, can the standard group consensus approach show that it has a reliable way to judge whether some potential answer stands the "best chance of being true"? (Supporters of the approach might otherwise hope to argue that it can accommodate a requirement for rigorous and thorough analysis.) Can an alternative hypothesis testing approach show that it can actually determine the potential answer (hypothesis) that has the "best chance of being true?"

There are two basic ways to make the needed comparison: (1) the answer could be compared all by itself against some absolute standard; or (2) it could be compared against other answers claiming to be valid (with or without an absolute standard).

Because for intelligence analysts the proven truth would not yet be known—and would obviate the whole probability exercise if it were—there is no evident absolute standard for comparison. This means that if there is but a single candidate to be the valid answer—such as supporters of group consensus would be inclined to put forward—judging it in any reasonably reliable way would be very difficult at best. What exactly would the single candidate answer be measured against, to see whether it has a strong or weak claim to be valid?

However, as students everywhere know, even if it is not feasible for grading to be conducted to an absolute standard (say, achieving a classroom test score of 100 percent), effective testing is still possible provided there are other competitors—which is good news for the alternative hypothesis testing approach. With other students competing, individual performances on a test can then be graded on a curve.[6]

Thus, a valid answer can stand the "best chance" of being true not by being compared against some absolute standard, which as noted seems impractical in intelligence analysis. Rather, it can stand the "best chance" of being true because it tests out better than other potential answers—or, more formally, hypotheses. As to what this grading should be based on: as emphasized above, it can only be how the hypotheses stack up when rigorous and thorough analysis is applied that covers both their data support and reasoning.

The bottom line, when the basics of intelligence analysis are pursued to their logical conclusion, is straightforward and inescapable—**the comparison of hypotheses must be a central concern for intelligence analysts**.

To sum up, the logic of intelligence analysis reflecting the basics considers in turn:

1   the analysts' professional responsibility to give policymakers a heads up and to be rigorous;
2   the nature of analysis that requires analysts to cover both data and reasoning in order to be thorough;
3   the analysts' inability to empirically verify their potential answer is true in time to give policymakers a heads up;
4   the consequent requirement to rely on probability to find the answer that stands the best chance of being true;
5   the lack of good intelligence performance records to address probability, which makes rigorous and thorough analysis of what is available in a current case particularly important;
6   the critical practical need, resulting from the lack of an absolute standard to gauge probability, to compare various hypotheses in order to determine the hypothesis that stands the best chance of being true; and appropriately
7   the ranking of these hypotheses based on the relative strengths and weaknesses of their data support and reasoning.

Overall, intelligence analysts have mixed messages. They cannot obtain certain **truth** for policymakers in time, but they can provide sound and timely **probability** judgments. The big challenge is actually doing the hypothesis testing to get those judgments. The logic of intelligence analysis makes clear there is no viable alternative. The common intelligence practice of looking to group consensus to yield the most probable answer is inadequate.

As a final point, since intelligence organizations routinely associate themselves with the pursuit of truth—no one, for example, ever says "probability" will make you free—it bears emphasizing that even the most rigorous and thorough hypothesis testing may not come up with an answer that eventually turns out to be true, when the real world's verdict comes in.

Hypothesis testing to determine probability is necessary not only because empirical verification is out of reach when analysts and policymakers most need it. Hypothesis testing is also called for because the data that analysts have to work with is generally less than ideal. As discussed below, it is not usually real "smoking gun" or "slam dunk" quality evidence. Such evidence, by itself, would pretty much get at the truth without analysts having to figure out how to piece it together with other evidence to make the most sense of it—which is the basic job of all-source analysts. Moreover, the hypothesis testing process itself leaves room for error. Even with a meticulously constructed testing process, intelligence analysts still face an obstacle that even bettors on horse races or on most election outcomes do not have to surmount. Unlike those bettors, intelligence analysts cannot count on the eventual winner (in this case, the hypothesis that turns out to be true) at least being among the contenders that they are comparing. It simply may not have been considered. Testing many hypotheses can improve the odds that the correct answer has been included but it is not fool proof.

Some special challenges for alternative hypothesis testing

To get the most out of alternative hypothesis testing, my method helps intelligence analysts address a number of challenges, which group consensus either has not effectively dealt with or, in many cases, even acknowledged as real concerns. My method's rule of thumb is: lacking an absolute standard to guide one's efforts, it generally makes sense to err on the side of doing too much rather than too little to come up with the most probable answer.

1 The challenge of dealing with analyst motives and biases

For intelligence analysts, there probably would be general acceptance that when colleagues offer different explanations on some issue, testing them as hypotheses seems sensible to see who can make the strongest case. Less easy to accept, however, is that a given analyst on his or her own should also be diligent in seeking out and evaluating alternatives to the explanation to which he or she is inclined. Why? For one thing, it can help put some inevitable questions to rest.

It is understandable for questions to arise about an analyst's motives or biases in determining whether his or her explanation holds up. This partly derives from the well-known concern about the "politicization" of intelligence, involving analysts being motivated to push a particular explanation due to pressures from some higher ups. Alternative hypothesis testing helps to put this and other motive issues in perspective. Such testing is all about judging explanations on their merits. If a favored explanation does not win out, then, whatever the motives behind it, no harm is done. If, on the other hand, the favored explanation tests out better than alternative explanations, it frankly doesn't matter whether it was even pushed for bad motives. Compared to its competitors, it still stands the best chance of being true and should be treated accordingly.

Therefore, just being able to turn to a tough testing process is a big help for an analyst. Provided the analyst is willing to risk submitting his or her favored explanation to alternative hypothesis testing, questions about one's motives can be made largely irrelevant. And if the motive concern is really a big issue on some important topic, the analyst might ask for outside reviewers to scrutinize such testing. (In general, my method strongly urges the participation of outside reviewers, particularly on important topics, to lend expertise and help ensure objectivity as hypothesis testing proceeds. Using such experts in a "pre mortem" role to avert bad analyses, as opposed to using them mainly in post mortems to pinpoint where finished analyses came up short, as has been common practice, simply makes sense.)

As for an analyst's personal biases, everyone has certain innate predispositions, interests, aversions and the like that are bound to affect the data one includes in an analysis and how one evaluates it—including the very important issue of how one weights individual bodies of data.[7] In covering the essential elements of analysis concerning reasoning, the alternative hypothesis testing in my method aims to <u>realistically</u> identify and remedy such cognitive biases, particularly calling for analysts to make their underlying assumptions explicit.[8]

2 The challenge of effectively assessing the real strengths and weaknesses of alternative hypotheses

Beyond helping to defang motive and bias concerns, the overriding reason an analyst should conduct alternative hypothesis testing is that sheer logic simply requires it. But is an analyst likely to appreciate the logic? Potential questions about one's motives and biases are only one set of considerations that an analyst must deal with in doing his or her job. The overall incentive structure of the work place matters a lot. Is serious consideration of alternative explanations really encouraged? It was not when I was still working. Is testing—any testing, not just alternative hypothesis testing—required or even valued? Again, not when I was still working.

In a work place governed by an incentive structure shaped by a group consensus approach to determining validity, none of this should be surprising. So let's walk through the analytic process as an analyst might normally experience it and see where he or she is confronted with key decisions about dealing with alternatives. Then one can better appreciate what the logic of intelligence analysis requires.

In deciding whether or not to push a favored explanation, an analyst must first consider whether the favored explanation is backed by truly compelling (i.e., real "smoking gun" or real "slam dunk" quality) evidence. But such evidence is rare. And, without it, there is always some possibility the explanation is wrong. If an analyst, therefore, appreciates the evidence in hand is less than compelling, the likely initial reaction would be to look for more evidence to try to buttress the favored explanation. Then the analyst would be expected to run the case by various colleagues (including "coordinating" with analysts with related expertise in other offices) to see if it is plausible and also submit it to one's manager to review. From there, in some version, it would be sent further up the bureaucratic chain of command to secure sign-offs that would finally make it official, "finished" intelligence. From my experience, this is a pretty typical line of march.

What is missing from this scenario is any real appreciation by the analyst that <u>if truly compelling evidence is lacking to support one view, it logically implies not only that the view could be wrong but that some other view could be right</u>. In other words, the need to seriously consider alternatives should be an immediate consideration for an analyst. And this is unlikely to happen in a work environment in which the incentive structure for analysts (and their managers) is shaped by a group consensus approach that does not encourage weighing of alternatives to determine validity.

Suppose, by contrast, that the analyst is attentive to giving alternative explanations a fair shake. In a nutshell, following the logic of intelligence analysis, once the analyst appreciates that the favored explanation is not supported by truly compelling evidence, the following sequence applies: (a) the analyst cannot wait for empirical verification to see if the favored explanation is true; (b) the analyst's only option is to find out whether the favored explanation actually <u>stands the best chance of being true</u> (i.e., is valid or least likely to be wrong); (c) but "best chance" according to what standard? Ideally, it should be the truth itself but no such comparison is feasible. So, practically, it has to be the "best chance" compared to other potential explanations—other hypotheses; (d) the analyst, thus, must come up with some alternative hypotheses to the favored hypothesis and compare all of them using some fair criteria (or metrics) to see which makes the strongest case.

But this is only the bare bones of needed analysis.

To be most effective, analysts should try to conduct alternative hypothesis testing that both uses multiple hypotheses and judges them by various tough criteria. In Chapter 3, I show that while doing this can be challenging, it is nevertheless practical for working analysts using the various testing techniques my method provides. For example, I illustrate in the hypothetical case study in Chapter 3 (which is a sanitized composite drawn from real life cases) the importance of using a number of alternative hypotheses rather than just one or two.[9] The favored hypothesis there is supported by a certain main body of data. If one alternative hypothesis was also supported by it, the favored hypothesis would still have a 50–50 chance to be correct based on this data—perhaps tolerable odds for some analysts. But I show that at least seven alternative hypotheses are compatible with this data. Hence, the favored hypothesis is not only weaker than originally assumed, but much weaker. In fact, when the testing is completed, the favored hypothesis emerges as the weakest of the contenders, because the seven others have better support from other data. *In other words, there is a complete turnaround in its fortunes.*

The flaws illustrated here underscore why the basics—both data and reasoning—need to be covered in a case. The favored explanation did not take into account all the relevant data. But poor reasoning fostered this. It was wrongly assumed that this was the only explanation consistent with the body of data that mattered. Why then even look for other data?

Overall, almost any alternative hypothesis testing is likely to be a big help for analysts. But significant refinements are still needed for such testing to be truly effective in determining how strong or how weak one's initially favored explanation really is—and whether it should be supplanted. In particular, as I learned in developing my method, this requires special efforts to try to ensure: (1) relevant hypotheses and their supporting data are not overlooked; and (2) relevant criteria for judging them (such as for shared consistency and not just inconsistency) are taken into account.

3 The challenge of encouraging group consensus to incorporate at least some testing in its procedures

Notwithstanding its benefits, alternative hypothesis testing still must contend with a powerful rival in intelligence for imposing quality control on analyses. That rival, as earlier discussed, is group consensus, which can take various forms. It can involve, as noted, securing a succession of sign-offs from officials in the chain of command in a given agency. It also can be the collective judgment of key officials from various agencies, convened to represent the IC.

In whatever form, group consensus makes a judgment based on a vote that a given explanation "stands the best chance of being true." This does not mean an analyst's proffered explanation is simply rubber stamped by reviewing officials. If that were the case, group consensus hardly would have been viewed as a legitimate quality control mechanism over the years. Critiques certainly occur and, in making them, a given official may sometimes suggest a better explanation. Nevertheless, this is still a far cry from a formalized testing process that starts with an analyst or analysts, makes a point of positing alternative explanations, and stipulates various criteria for comparing them. As earlier discussed, such testing is not fool proof but <u>enables analysts to realistically do the best they can</u> in coming up with sound probability judgments for policymakers.

Adopting alternative hypothesis testing, however, would not fundamentally change the bureaucratic arrangements that have pertained to group consensus. What would be different is that analysts would have to provide reviewing officials with an actual test and these officials would then have to scrutinize it. In a sense, both analysts and officials would still "vote" to claim validity for a proposed explanation, but the driver of the process would be the testing that produces this explanation in the first place.

Since group consensus does not encourage comparison of alternative explanations, testing per se is understandably less important for it. Still, by determining validity through a vote <u>without a test to back it up</u>, group consensus winds up being starkly at odds with what the logic of intelligence analysis requires to obtain a valid explanation—namely, rigorous and thorough testing.

Running at least *some* serious test of the favored explanation view before voting on it would seem merely prudent and thus should be routine. But, in observing group consensus in action over many years in intelligence analysis, I almost never saw analysts or reviewing officials call for such testing. A test of this sort is certainly feasible. My method incorporates it as a "zero-based review" of a dominant view's (i.e., favored explanation's) data support and reasoning. (The review starts with a simple, 10 question "basic scrub" of a dominant view's underpinnings that alone can be helpful.) The test faces supporters of group consensus with a risk-reward situation. On the one hand, a zero-based review can reveal whether a dominant view is basically sound and thus sensible to vote for. On the other hand, it might show the view is badly flawed, which would then make a strong argument for considering alternative explanations.[10]

To underscore the utility of a zero-based review, in Chapter 2 I draw on the unclassified version of the official U.S. post mortem on the major intelligence failure on Iraqi WMD. The post mortem said: "When we reviewed finished intelligence, we found egregious examples of poor tradecraft, such as using a piece of evidence to support an argument when the same piece supported exactly the opposite argument—and failing to note this fact."[11] Obviously, detecting such analytic flaws <u>before</u> they make it into finished intelligence would be highly desirable. A proper zero-based review—functioning in effect as a "pre mortem"—can help do that.

As it is, both by giving alternatives short shrift and neglecting testing, group consensus must be rated—as the logic of intelligence analysis indicates—as inadequate to secure sound probability judgments. And all of this compounds its major failing that it provides no reliable standard to judge what would constitute the most probable answer in the first place.

Despite the longstanding dominance of group consensus, alternative hypothesis testing should still have made more headway in intelligence analysis by now—at least by being used on particularly important or difficult issues. But, as earlier emphasized, in my experience in the business for almost three decades hypothesis testing lingered on the periphery.

Although some progress may have been made since then, I do not believe there has been a recent sea change. Indeed, even for the most important intelligence issues that are assessed in U.S. National Intelligence Estimates (NIEs), serious hypothesis testing does not appear to have caught on. NIEs acknowledge some dissents but still treat them as but footnotes to mainstream views. This has long been standard practice. I witnessed it first hand as a drafter and manager of a number of NIEs, dating back to those on Soviet strategic forces during the heyday of the Cold War.

So, if one is looking to explain why intelligence failures occur, a lack of appreciation that, when empirical verification is out of reach, probability must be rigorously and thoroughly addressed is a good place to start.

4 The challenge of transparency

In intelligence, transparency of one's method should be the natural companion of rigorous and thorough analysis (this does not include making secrets public), since the aim is to persuade one's audiences. They comprise other analysts, managers in the bureaucratic chain of command, and pertinent policymakers including military commanders.

In my analyses, I have operated on the premise that the data and reasoning that persuade me that a given hypothesis stands the best chance of being true (i.e., is valid) should be made as clear as possible to all audiences. For example, I have devised easy to understand test charts, comparing data support for the competing hypotheses, that make individual hypotheses' strengths and weaknesses readily apparent. Hypotheses are also ranked on a numerical basis, avoiding the ambiguity of using qualitative discriminators that dub some hypotheses "possible," others "probable," and yet others "highly likely."[12]

Unfortunately, my approach runs contrary to an intelligence predisposition to boil down the justifications for various judgments, especially for the powerful, on the premise that important people lack the time (and often the background) to thoroughly consider certain detailed arguments. On minor issues this might be reasonable, but not when quite important threat or other major intelligence issues are at stake. Here, however, U.S. NIEs typically employ a fallback. To complement the data and reasoning deemed appropriate for policymakers, NIEs invoke the authority of the collective wisdom of the multiple agencies. Their group consensus underpins the call that the IC has "high" or some other level of confidence in a given judgment.

While the IC's confidence call may be good for policymakers to know, they should not be expected to simply be swayed by it—especially for "high confidence" judgments. Certainly on any major issue, policymakers also should be afforded (consistent of course with security sensitivities) data and reasoning that are clearly laid out and supported with sufficient detail to be persuasive in their own right. Why is this necessary? Without being provided with a case that can stand on its own, policymakers obviously will lack the means to make a properly informed and responsible decision as to whether in fact they share the IC's level of confidence.

It is bad enough when analyses are much less rigorous and thorough than they should be and eschew testing—and, moreover, lack a reliable standard of probability by which they can be judged. But when this set of deficiencies is combined with a "just trust the professionals" culture, key intelligence consumers suffer a double blow. There is not only a greater chance of intelligence failures, but—notwithstanding the occasional "low confidence" call in estimates—key consumers are less likely to see them coming.

Transparency also poses a special challenge for computerized statistical probability analysis, because this analysis depends on sophisticated mathematical calculations that only math and computer whizzes truly understand. (I admit that I am not one of them.) The demand for deference from audiences who lack such expertise is thus built into its use in intelligence and other endeavors.

Even in a "just trust the professionals" culture, this may be an excessive demand. If computerized statistical probability analysis is to become a viable threat analysis tool in the future, major efforts will be needed to make it more transparent. This is required to enable a substantial cadre of working analysts to use it. Relying on an "elite" corps of math and computer gurus would inadequately cover the range of intelligence issues and, at best, relegate other analysts to research assistant status.[13]

Furthermore, without transparency, non expert policymakers will be reluctant to base life and death decisions on a threat analysis they cannot really understand.

5   The challenge of prioritizing "managing analytic flaws" over "managing uncertainties" to make hypothesis testing a practical prediction tool

Meeting all the previous challenges is ultimately intended to help altern-ative hypothesis testing work as a means to obtain intelligence answers that "stand the best chance of being true." As the logic of intelligence ana-lysis emphasizes, obtaining such valid answers is the best analysts can be expected to do in making predictions for policymakers. Probability (valid-ity), not certainty (truth), is what they can provide.

At least in the modern era, a guiding principle for addressing (and improving) probabilities has been for analysts of all sorts to try to "manage uncertainties." Once one accepts that uncertainties can be reduced not eliminated, this principle seems sensible on its face. But in intelligence analysis it is not a practical guide for hypothesis testing—for finding the hypothesis that stands the best chance of being true.

I have taken as my method's guide the synonym for a hypothesis that "stands the best chance of being true": namely, the hypothesis that "is least likely to be wrong." Accordingly, I focus on analytic flaws that can make a probability judgment wrong. At least 10 key flaws can undercut intelligence predictions. These flaws comprise: inconsistencies; shared consistencies; leaving key assumptions unexamined; discounting adversary behavior that seems irrational but isn't; overlooking relevant hypotheses (for various reasons); overlooking relevant available data (for various reasons); poor weighting of data; and flaws encouraged by foreign D&D—ignoring (or poorly assessing) missing data and using phony data.

Before explaining how focusing on such flaws serves policymakers better than focusing on "managing uncertainties," some background is appropriate.

Over the centuries, rulers have used various mechanisms to try to look into the future—such as oracles for the ancient Greeks, augurs to read animal entrails and the flight patterns of birds for the ancient Romans, and a perennial favorite even in modern times, astrologers to get celestial insights. But the job has been hard. Indeed, one modern scholar has made a point of exploring why some things are simply impossible to predict.[14]

Still, if gauging probabilities was generally a feckless exercise, insur-ance companies and other enterprises with a strong stake in knowing the odds would be out of business. Therefore, even for those who have shied away from serious efforts at statistical probability analysis but still have an institutional responsibility to predict, which is generally the case for intelligence organizations, it has at least been respectable to urge their analysts to "manage uncertainties." But from a practical standpoint—even though this may seem heretical to some academics and others who calculate probabilities as a profession—I do not believe managing uncertainties should be an intelligence analyst's priority concern.

Uncertainties, to be sure, make threat or other intelligence prediction difficult enough, because they risk making predictions inaccurate. But, importantly, they do not predetermine inaccuracy. By their nature, uncertainties can wind up undercutting a prediction, breaking in its favor, or having little or no effect on it. My method therefore urges analysts to have as their first priority "managing analytic flaws" that cause errors— thereby trying to minimize errors—because these flaws can seriously compound the <u>risk</u> of inaccuracy that uncertainties pose. In short, just as physicians are admonished to first "do no harm," analysts should first avoid making the prediction problem worse.

Put another way, compared to managing uncertainties, managing analytic flaws that cause errors merits priority concern because it is simply a more practical and realistic way to tackle the prediction problem in intelligence. In the context of alternative hypothesis testing, finding the hypothesis that stands the best chance of being true (i.e., is valid) is, as noted, the same as coming up with the hypothesis that is least likely to be wrong. And analytic errors obviously contribute to a hypothesis being wrong.

Managing uncertainties, of course, also aims to improve the odds that a given hypothesis is valid. A key difference is that managing analytic flaws is something over which analysts have considerable control. Whereas relevant uncertainties in a given case are not only harder to ameliorate but harder to identify in the first place, the hypothesis testing in my method identifies a range of analytic flaws. Equally important, it also shows analysts how to use various techniques—and provides step by step guidance in a case study—to remedy them.

In dealing with analytic flaws, my method is aided by paying close attention to the basic components of analysis with their essentials discussed above. To be as thorough as possible, it systematically seeks out flaws across the spectrum of essentials: that is, flaws that can affect the quantity of data, the quality of data, and the soundness of one's assumptions and train of logic. Further, I urge analysts to be on the lookout for any other flaws as they apply the method. They can be helped as well by working through the essentials of analysis checklist. (Readers can get the best sense of the overall checklist in Chapter 4. To provide guidance for computerized statistical probability analysis as a future intelligence tool, I summarize in sequence each key flaw and how my method remedies/ manages it.)

Since my method does not presuppose that uncertainties simply go away, it advises analysts to tackle them also, when it is possible to do so. But here intelligence analysts have some substantial disadvantages, which underscore why managing uncertainties is not a prudent first priority.

Besides having less control over uncertainties than they do over producing flawed analyses, analysts face serious deficiencies in dealing with uncertainties in intelligence analysis. Unlike dealing with analytic errors, where there is at least a baseline of useful guidance to build on (Heuer's methodology underscoring the importance of inconsistencies as a key flaw is a prime example), there is nothing comparable for managing uncertainties. This has not kept intelligence organizations from echoing scholarly sentiments that managing uncertainties is important—probably because it seems eminently sensible when one is trying to predict something. But (at least when I was still working), there has been no useful follow up. Urgings to manage uncertainties have not been accompanied by practical guidance—for example, a case study or studies—to show analysts step by step how they should go about it.

Probably an even more significant drawback for analysts is the lack of good intelligence performance records, particularly those covering intelligence successes. If good records of successes were available, analysts could draw on them to see how uncertainties were handled in the past. Almost certainly uncertainties were encountered and, since successes were registered anyhow, obviously they were somehow dealt with effectively. That is, they were somehow "managed."

The lack of good performance records also affects an analyst's ability to deal with one of the central issues for managing uncertainty: weighting bodies of data that bear on a probability judgment, something of concern to any serious analyst or methodologist trying to calculate probabilities. This is a tough problem in the best of circumstances. But if one has solid data on analogous past cases, there is at least a reasonable chance of reducing uncertainty about how bodies of data should be weighted in a current case. How did comparable bodies of data impact on the outcome of those cases in the past?

Without decent performance records, particularly on past successes, none of this potential help for intelligence analysts to try to "manage uncertainties" is available.

All of this, unfortunately, seems to reflect the fact that intelligence organizations often fool themselves as well as others when they tout big goals that they are pursuing. A common mantra for intelligence organizations has been to call on their analysts to "learn best practices"—which, if these organizations are serious about it, presumably would include "best practices" for pursuing the important goal of managing uncertainties. But without solid and detailed records on past intelligence successes, it is hard to see what analysts could realistically draw on to make this happen.

In sum, in yet another intelligence irony, while analysts are not only dutifully reminded to "manage uncertainties" but entreated as well to "learn best practices," the resources to support such efforts have been meager at best. Therefore, even though managing analytic flaws may seem a secondary issue to some professional calculators of probabilities, it is at least a sensible—rather than an impractical—way to tackle the prediction problem in intelligence.[15]

Whether using computerized statistical probability analysis, with sophisticated mathematical modeling, would offer better prospects for dealing with the uncertainties affecting threat and other intelligence prediction remains to be seen. Certainly, the chance that it might would be a strong selling point for transferring its use from the civilian world to intelligence in the future.

Nevertheless, given that intelligence attention to past performances (particularly successes) has been deficient, computerized statistical probability analysis could not fruitfully employ one of its longstanding empirical supports for civilian probability calculations—performance records. It is here that the expertise of its gurus would be particularly needed: to select (or devise) a technique (or techniques) that would compensate for the lack of appropriate records.

Furthermore, computerized statistical probability analysis would still have to deal with the impact of analytic error. Thus, a basic selling point for my own method is that its focus on analytic error can (as noted) provide essential guidance to help sophisticated mathematical modeling do the job in the future.

6 The overall challenge of competing with group consensus: how alternative hypothesis testing employed in my method compares

The logic of intelligence analysis, as laid out earlier, provides only the bare bones of needed analysis and concludes that, on that basis alone, group consensus is inadequate to secure sound probability judgments. The various challenges then discussed help to flesh out those bare bones to show that, in order to qualify for widespread acceptance in intelligence analysis, alternative hypothesis testing has work to do of its own. And that is what I have designed my method to accomplish.

So, overall, how do alternative hypothesis testing as reflected in my method and the longstanding group consensus approach ultimately compare? Here's a brief summary. Neither approach has access to the truth, but alternative hypothesis testing nevertheless:

1   provides a standard to judge probability—group consensus does not;
2   makes alternative explanations a central concern—group consensus does not;
3   helps defang "politicization" and other motive and bias issues—group consensus does not;
4   can rigorously and thoroughly compare various alternative explanations— group consensus basically opts for a vote on a single explanation without any testing;
5   is transparent—group consensus is not;
6   can be a practical prediction tool by focusing on managing analytic errors—group consensus (to the extent it follows traditional and oft touted guidance) would likely focus on managing uncertainties, which is impractical in intelligence analysis.

The case for alternative methodology testing

Since my method is principally intended for working intelligence analysts dealing with cases that are classified, I am not in a position as a retired intelligence officer (without active clearances) to benefit from what analysts might have learned about whether the method has helped them and, in particular, where it needs fixing. In any event, the basic presentation of the method has been available for about six years and publishing statistics indicate that it, and my follow up articles, have enjoyed substantial circulation.

Even without analyst feedback, however, I think it useful to suggest a quality check on my method that I have not previously proposed but believe to be eminently logical. Namely, subject the method to what might be called a "comparative methodology review." Especially for methodologists proposing methods hinging on the use of alternative hypotheses, it would be hypocritical to contend in a given case that one's own methodology is the only way to go. Maybe other methodologies can do the job better.

But—in accord with the very standards that the logic of intelligence analysis sets—the comparative value of any given methodology for intelligence analysis cannot be determined by: how widely it is used (such as group consensus); nor by book or article sales; nor by the plaudits or critical reviews of other scholars or intelligence professionals. None of these can come close to what the real world's verdict might reveal. Did a predicted event occur or not? That is ultimately the judgment that counts.

A methodology with an eye toward the coming demands of the digital age, which merits serious consideration, has been advanced by Professor Philip Tetlock. Unimpressed by the track records of various experts in making predictions, after he extensively studied them, Tetlock focuses on identifying and cultivating certain mental attitudes that he believes improve the odds for making successful predictions.[16] Since there clearly are differences in imagination, curiosity, mental powers of association and the like among individuals in almost any group, some would be expected to be better at predicting than others. Individuals with the best prospects for success (whom Tetlock dubs "superforecasters") presumably would exhibit a special talent—a natural "feel"—for analysis. Among intelligence analysts, I would call them modern day, incipient Sherlock Holmes types, given the famous sleuth's exceptional observational and deductive skills.

Because of the span and variety of intelligence issues, however, there is a significant practical question to be addressed: where would these "elite" analysts fit? Rank and file analysts would still have to cover the vast bulk of intelligence issues, and they are therefore the basic audience for my method. It aims overall to help them do their job better—with training that involves rigorous, thorough, and transparent hypothesis testing. Taking over this big job from these analysts, and doing it even better, would clearly require a lot of incipient Sherlocks. And if that were somehow possible, what then would the rest of the intelligence analysts do?

It seems more practical to try to combine different approaches for improving intelligence analysis. For example, analysts first trained in my method, and demonstrating that they are particularly adept in implementing it, would be a natural talent pool for a Sherlock search to target.[17] Once identified, their skills could then be honed further, drawing on Tetlock's insights. These analysts would be valuable mentors for other analysts (who, after all, would have shared their original training) and a source of expertise to be tapped on particularly tough or important intelligence issues.

But whether or not some combination of the two methods could be arranged, Professor Tetlock's approach would be important to test in its own right in a comparative methodology review. How well would it actually do on its own? How well would my methodology do? Or any other methodologies that might be put forward—including, in particular, the longstanding group consensus approach?

The only way to find out is to have individual analysts or teams compete by using my method and some other method (or methods) of their choosing to address the <u>same</u> intelligence issue—a "live" issue where the real world's verdict is not yet known and where a predictive judgment is required. Here even empirical verification that is necessarily tardy might bear some real fruit. That is, once the eventual real world outcome is known, the analysts can see which method did best. Then they should do all the necessary forensics to try to figure out why, and draw the appropriate lessons for the competing methodologies. Finally, in accord with the scientific dictum that the results of experiments should be repeatable, the same drill should be performed on other cases.[18]

This "real world" testing procedure is a sensible response to those with a strong skepticism about formal methodologies (such as Professor Tetlock himself) as the way to improve intelligence or other prediction. This skepticism is understandable and is particularly likely to come into play for intelligence practitioners leery of the utility of digital age methodologies that feature sophisticated mathematical modeling. The basic attitude here is exemplified in the fairly common "I told you so" rejoinders when some meteorology model gets the track of a hurricane wrong. But those who wish to cite such digital age glitches in order to sustain the group consensus approach in intelligence[19] cannot really duck the test outlined above. It invites any prognosticators, with whatever formal or informal practices for making predictions, to put their favorite approach on the line. If a better arbiter exists than the real world outcome, I am not aware of it.

Chances for change?

Prediction is the principal mission of intelligence collection and analysis and, in Tetlock's words, prediction can be taught. The priority of prediction for intelligence sometimes gets obscured because policymakers also require accurate assessments of what is currently happening in the world.[20] The attack on Pearl Harbor stands as a strong reminder of what intelligence priorities really are. It made them crystal clear on that grim Sunday morning. As the attack was unfolding, getting accurate current updates of the carnage was of course an important intelligence concern. And, to be sure, after the fact there was still a pressing intelligence concern to see whether similar attacks were likely elsewhere. But it would be hard to dispute that the intelligence mission that ranked way above all was predicting the attack in the first place.

Realistically, however, the mission of prediction for intelligence analysis is not to pursue the chimera of regularly achieving pinpoint accuracy. That was conceded long ago when U.S. intelligence opted to call its big predictions for policymakers "estimates"—which connote providing what is essentially a ball park heads up, rather than something more precise and measurable. But something more precise and measurable is still possible if the requirements of determining probabilities are taken into account. They could have been taken into account over the years, better than they have been, with techniques that call for hypothesis testing. They certainly will have to be confronted when digital age mathematical modeling techniques make an increasingly strong case for getting in the game. And, as I have tried to show, at least some techniques for dealing with probabilities are, after all, "teachable."

So, what can my method contribute? Overall, against the backdrop of the many proposals and approaches advanced over the years for improving intelligence analysis (including in the following chapters in this hand-book), I have offered two more:

1   confront the traditional commitment to group consensus with a straightforward logical layout of the roots of knowledge in intelligence analysis—it argues for hypothesis testing and shows group consensus to be inadequate; and
2   urge intelligence practitioners to make a concerted effort to gain acceptance of the only true test of whether one or another approach works best—this is a comparison of how these approaches fare, when the jury comes in, in assessing and predicting the same real world intelligence issue.

Will these new proposals, in addition to those already on the books, make a difference? This will depend entirely on whether, in the ranks of today's analysts, managers, and other concerned intelligence officials, these proposals are viewed as useful ammunition to argue in house for significant changes. And why might these individuals be concerned enough to do that? Hopefully, because they would appreciate not only that current intelligence analysis can be improved but that these changes would be a necessary first step in preparing intelligence analysis for the much more fundamental adjustments that the digital age will require.

Notes

1   For example, in the 1970s there was a brief flurry of interest among Sovietologists in trying to apply Graham Allison's innovative ideas on decision making to Soviet policymaking. (I was among them and, as an analyst then at the Institute for Defense Analyses, tried to promote these ideas in my *Analyzing Soviet Strategic Arms Decisions*, Westview Press, Boulder, CO, 1978.) The flurry, however, did not make any big dent in intelligence analysis. Professor Allison's 1971 book, *Essence of Decision: Explaining the Cuban Missile Crisis* (and a later update and revision [1999]), can be found on the Internet.

2 A prime example of the shortcomings of the big post mortems is that, in an effort to encourage more attention to alternative views in analysis (in my opinion, obviously a commendable objective), both supported the idea of setting up "red cells" in intelligence organizations. On a given intelligence issue, these red cells would be tasked with coming up with explanations that are outside the box. By itself, however, this set up can lead to a free-for-all of speculation. For alternatives to be taken seriously, they need to be compared against each other, as well as against the prevailing conventional wisdom, in some real testing. In the case of the 9/11 attacks, Richard Clarke, President George W. Bush's counter terrorism advisor, clearly appreciated the inadequacy of just laying out various alternatives. According to the *Report of the National Commission on Terrorist Attacks Upon the United States*: "In his testimony, Clarke commented that he thought that warning about the possibility of a suicide hijacking would have been just one more speculative theory among many ..." See the full final report: www.9-11commission.gov/report/911Report.pdf, p. 345.

   Clarke's continuing concern with warning is most recently reflected in his book, with R.P. Eddy, aimed at identifying individuals in various fields who are particularly good at it, whom he dubs "Cassandras." See his *Warnings: Finding Cassandras to Stop Catastrophes*, Harper Collins, New York, 2017.

   Insightful comments on the pros and cons of the Iraqi WMD post mortem can be found in Robert Jervis, *Why Intelligence Fails: Lessons from the Iranian Revolution and the Iraq War*, Cornell University Press, Ithaca, NY, 2010.

3 Having dealt with issues of epistemology at some length in my Ph.D. dissertation on political theory (*The Intellectual Imperative: Hegel's Response to Kant*, Harvard University, Cambridge, MA, 1974), I am well aware that professional epistemologists are likely to view this presentation as quite rudimentary. But that is the point. What matters is whether intelligence professionals (analysts, their supervisors, and others), intimately familiar with what their profession involves, buy into the straightforward assertions/propositions and the sequence of argumentation that results in the basic conclusion. (Time worn epistemological issues, by the way, lie at the heart of the big intelligence problem of "connecting the dots," made famous by the 9/11 attacks. See Chapter 2, p. 38 and Chapter 2, note 10).

4 All-source analysts have a function, in the first place, basically because collectors only occasionally obtain secrets that are truly "smoking gun" (or "slam dunk") quality. Such secrets need little interpretation or massaging (see also p. 9).

5 This characterization of intelligence performance records may come as news for many readers. But from personal experience, I can attest that no analysts, of whom I am aware, regarded these records to be comprehensive enough or sufficiently detailed and balanced to serve as a reliable underpinning for making probability judgments on a current case. For more discussion of intelligence performance records, see the section in Chapter 4 entitled: "Big data on intelligence performance: where is it?"

6 The example of a typical classroom setting is useful to illuminate the relationship between having an absolute standard and having to rely on a competition to determine what "stands the best chance" of being true. As any student who has taken a test in which a grade of 100 percent is possible knows, a single student can be graded in such a test but multiple students also can be graded.

When multiple students are graded, a given student's performance is therefore judged against the absolute standard—e.g., the student may get a grade of 90 percent—and compared as well against the performances of other students. They may get either better, worse, or the same percentage grades on the test.

But sometimes an instructor may decide that the nature of the subject matter does not make setting an absolute standard practical or desirable (such as when easily measurable true or false test questions or multiple choice test questions cannot be used). Then grading on a curve in which students' performances are simply compared against each other is the instructor's only recourse—which is also the case for intelligence analysis.

Moreover, in intelligence analysis whether or not to set an absolute standard is hardly a matter of discretion for some instructor. In a typical classroom setting, an instructor can decide what represents the "truth" in some subject matter for testing—what, in effect, would merit a grade of 100 percent. So the instructor can obviously know what the "truth" is before testing commences. In intelligence analysis, no analysts or their supervisors can know what the truth really is until it is too late to meet the crucial intelligence requirement of giving policymakers a needed heads up.

7 Weighting can have a major impact on the integrity of any analysis that brings different bodies of data to bear to determine probability. An analyst has essentially two weighting options: try to assign different weights to the bodies of data or treat them as having equal weight. Deliberately assigning different weights is often attempted but is very hard to implement effectively. It has the worthy objective of ensuring that an "important" body of data appropriately counts more than a "less important" counterpart in determining the outcome of an analysis. But the relative importance of such bodies of data often will not be self-evident in the first place and how much weight to actually assign them will be even less obvious. Because of these large uncertainties, cognitive biases are likely to have a significant impact. In particular, personal preferences (and sheer guesswork) cannot help but influence how weights are assigned. (This risk is compounded in intelligence analysis because analysts lack decent performance records, which would enable them to look to previous analogous cases to see how comparable bodies of data may have affected their outcomes. See also note 5.)

My method therefore opts for basically giving equal weight to all assessed inconsistencies and all critical missing data that constitute its validation tasks, which determine how hypotheses are ultimately ranked (see note 12 and discussion in Chapter 3, note 5). Equal weighting guards against making subjective judgments on the importance of a given body of data. It cannot, however, override the uncertainties inherent in weighting and firmly establish that all inconsistencies and missing data in fact have equal weight. Much more likely, equal weighting will undervalue some of them and overvalue others (although which ones will be affected and to what degree will remain indeterminate). Nevertheless, the impact of any distortions can be lessened, so that the basic integrity of the rankings is maintained, by trying to maximize the bodies of data used. This increases the chances that the bodies of data that may be overvalued and those that may be undervalued will tend to balance out.

8 To offer practical guidance in a methodology, one needs to be realistic about dealing with the cognitive biases that can affect an intelligence analyst's reasoning on a particular intelligence issue. As psychologist and Nobel prize

winner, Daniel Kahneman, has detailed in his book, *Thinking, Fast and Slow* (Farrar, Straus & Giroux, New York, 2011), such biases can affect an individual's thinking in many and varied ways. Dealing with these biases in intelligence analysis therefore will always be a work in progress.

But I believe my method gives analysts a good start in dealing with at least some of the most important cognitive biases—which, hopefully, will also prompt them to be attentive to other biases as they carry out their analyses. The alternative hypothesis testing in my method: (a) unlike the group consensus approach, obliges analysts to look at a given issue from different perspectives— that is, through a variety of "lenses"—not just from a favored (or even familiar) point of view; (b) strongly urges analysts to make their underlying assumptions explicit to see if they hold up; (c) as later discussed in the text, includes techniques (mainly by employing many hypotheses) to prudently stretch an analyst's imagination so that data that would otherwise be overlooked is included; (d) shows analysts how to have a nuanced perspective on adversary "irrationality" (particularly to tap the expertise of regional or country experts, to take into account behavior that may <u>seem</u> irrational in Western eyes but makes sense within its own cultural context. See also notes 15 and 17); and finally (e) as discussed in note 7, helps analysts minimize the impact of cognitive biases on their weighting of data.

9 I call the test that is illustrated here a "shared consistency" test, which is one of a number of tests I employ to compare hypotheses. Overall, my methodology uses various metrics to try to compare hypotheses as rigorously and thoroughly as possible. They are all presented and explained in Chapter 2. My main metric compares hypotheses as to which has the most and least inconsistencies with the relevant data in a given case. This inconsistency test is based on Karl Popper's refinements of the scientific method and Heuer's adaptation of Popper's approach for intelligence analysis. In contrast to both Popper and Heuer, however, I also compare hypotheses in terms of data that they fail to take into account—that is, missing data. One aim is to deal with the potential impact of foreign denial, which is not a real concern in academic hypothesis testing but is—or should be—a major concern for intelligence analysts. (In a given case, intelligence analysts first have to focus on what data is missing and then address why it may be missing. Its absence could mean an adversary is denying this data to them. Or it could mean that hypotheses for which it would be relevant simply lack this supporting data.)

10 Supporters of group consensus get a fair shake in a zero-based review, but the test is not a surrogate for being judged against an "absolute standard" as discussed in the logic of intelligence analysis. And, by its nature, it is not as rigorous as undergoing a comparison with alternative hypotheses. Still, it can help guard against making at least "egregious" errors, which is considerably better than undergoing no serious testing, which has been standard practice for group consensus approaches. By the same token, insofar as a zero-based review highlights the need for considering other potential answers, it can turn out to be particularly helpful for methodologists and analysts arguing for alternative hypothesis testing—simply from a practical standpoint. It might spell the difference between making headway or just spinning one's wheels in the work place, given that group consensus has long held sway there. Intelligence methodologists often do not give sufficient attention to what it will take for their methodology to take hold in the bureaucratic setting in which they intend it to

be used. For a methodology to be practical, it is important to appreciate that the "buy in" for using it as it is being taught in a supportive classroom setting may or may not be matched by a warm reception when the analyst returns to his or her work place.

11 See Internet site, Government Publishing Office, *Unclassified Version of the Report of the Commission on the Intelligence Capabilities of the United States Regarding Weapons of Mass Destruction*, March 31, 2005: www.gpo.gov/fdsys/pkg/GPO-WMD/pdf/GPO-WMD.pdf, p. 408.

12 As I show in presenting the results of the hypothetical case, featured in Chapter 3, I do comparisons that involve eight hypotheses, eight sets of available data, and five sets of critical missing data. I display these comparisons in easy to understand "inconsistency" and "missing data" test charts. Based on such testing, I compile tallies for each hypothesis of the bodies of relevant available data with which the hypothesis is inconsistent. I then compile tallies for each hypothesis of the bodies of critical data that are missing. The combined tallies—which I designate as "overall validation tasks"—are the basis for determining which of the hypotheses is "most likely," which is "least likely," and which fall in between. (The zero-based review and shared consistency testing are by no means left out of consideration. They feed into the major testing that determines the overall validation tasks.) Issues of weighting data and the like are dealt with in the analysis leading up to these concluding judgments. Justifications are presented in the text for why the various hypotheses and data sets qualify in the first place.

Analysts and their audiences are left with no ambiguity as to how a given hypothesis compares against its competitors, since the overall hypotheses and data sets are presented in concrete numbers and the inconsistencies and critical missing data for each hypothesis are presented in concrete numbers. These numbers do <u>not</u> translate, however, into a judgment that a given hypothesis has a certain percentage probability of being correct (see also note 6). To make such a judgment responsibly, analysts would also have to take into account the impact of uncertainties. And, as I make clear in the text, the lack of decent performance records (and other deficiencies) make it risky to claim that one can give intelligence analysts reliable guidance on how to do that. <u>Therefore, what I leave analysts with is simply this: based on the metrics I use, the numbers enable them to clearly and precisely inform both their bosses and policymakers which hypotheses are stronger or weaker and why.</u>

By contrast, on occasion intelligence organizations try to reduce the ambiguity of their qualitative judgments by using numbers, such as designating that "highly likely" means a probability of 90 percent. This might promote a common understanding among intelligence analysts, reviewing officials, and policymakers of what "highly likely" represents, but it can create the misleading impression that an actual quantification occurred that resulted in the 90 percent number. Key questions go begging, such as: "How did one arrive at that number?" "What exactly is it based on?" Satisfactory answers to these questions are unlikely to be forthcoming.

13 For widespread application in intelligence analysis, any formal or informal methodology must be accessible to rank and file analysts and not just be a tool that one needs special skills to use. Think of the problem as being similar to deciding whether or not to use a recipe for baking a cake. I believe that a recipe (a structured approach) maximizes the chances for a lot of

analysts to be able to "bake a decent cake." That is why I provided the hypothetical case study in Chapter 3 as an instructional aid for analysts. In it, I offer, in the appropriate sequence, step by step guidance for implementing each of the key techniques in my method—the zero-based review, the shared consistency test, the inconsistency test, and the missing data test—and cap it off with unambiguous quantitative tallies (described in note 12). Moreover, acknowledging the span and variety of intelligence issues, I urge analysts to make adaptations in any of these techniques as needed when tackling real world issues.

Some other methodologists (such as Professor Philip Tetlock, whose work I discuss later), have a different outlook on the value of recipes to "bake a cake." They are more inclined toward an unstructured approach, which offers some broad guidelines but puts a premium on fostering personal creativity and improvisational skills. However, the problem for any approach that relies on an analytic "elite"—which applies as well to Richard Clarke's recent book (see note 2)—is that this approach may enable certain analysts ("superforecasters" for Tetlock, "Cassandras" for Clarke) to sometimes "bake a superb cake," but it will not be enough to help other analysts turn out more than mediocre cakes. Broad guidelines simply will not equip rank and file analysts to deal effectively with a number of factors—such as foreign D&D and inadequate performance records—that are special to intelligence analysis and can foster analytic error in various ways.

The least productive option would be to require analysts to follow a recipe but then provide one in a foreign language only a few bakers can understand. This is essentially the situation that computerized statistical probability methods, with sophisticated mathematical modeling, will face. It is why major efforts will be needed to make these methods more transparent for intelligence analysts to use. For their part, intelligence analysts will have to do some work of their own if and when these digital age "recipes" are translated. Many analysts are likely to need serious training to improve their math skills, which training courses will in turn have to add to their curricula.

14 See the discussion of Nassim Taleb's "black swan" concept in Will Davies' review of Taleb's and other uses of this metaphor in the *Oxonian Review of Books*, Issue 6.3, June 2007.

15 Since "managing uncertainties" is generally acknowledged as the appropriate bumper sticker for anyone seriously interested in addressing probabilities, I appreciate that advocating a focus on "managing analytic flaws" calls for showing that it can provide significant help for intelligence analysts. Therefore, I try to cover the waterfront in identifying flaws that matter, particularly those that can affect both the hypotheses an analyst considers and the data and reasoning to evaluate them. Examples include:

1 What with all the bizarre, barbarous acts by terrorists, one would think intelligence analysts are by now fully sensitized to take into account all manner of "irrational" adversary behavior. Not so. Acutely irrational behavior, as reflected in extreme terrorist acts, is unlikely to be dismissed as implausible, certainly these days. Whereas other behavior that seems irrational in Western eyes, but is merely different from how Westerners would tackle the same problem, may well be left out of consideration. An analyst might, for example, ignore some source information on an adversary weapon program that, while technically feasible, seems "irrational" in terms of how the U.S.

would build such a weapon. Therefore, a hypothesis that the adversary is building this weapon might not even be included among the hypotheses that are being tested. Moreover, the supporting evidence is likely to be sidelined as well. To counter this flawed understanding of adversary behavior, my method helps analysts better appreciate the nuances of adversary "irrationality" and reflect this in their hypothesis testing (see also note 17).

2 The example in the text (drawn from the hypothetical case in Chapter 3) of the flawed assumption that only the favored hypothesis is consistent with a certain main body of data—when in fact seven other hypotheses are consistent with it—is a particularly dramatic example of poor reasoning that affects which hypotheses analysts consider and what data they use. If an analyst is only worried about avoiding <u>inconsistencies</u> and is not attentive to <u>shared consistencies,</u> this flaw can easily go unnoticed. As the quote in the text on "egregious examples of poor tradecraft" from the Iraqi WMD post mortem (see note 11 citation) makes clear, this flaw can also contribute to major intelligence failures. I know this to be so as well in another (still classified) real world case.

And how about that vexing problem of assigning weights to various bodies of evidence that one uses in an analysis, which can substantially affect whether the overall analysis is basically sound or badly skewed? If one approaches this problem from the standpoint of "managing uncertainties," a sensible standard technique to reduce uncertainty is to draw on previous analogous cases to see which types of data had a greater or lesser impact in determining their outcome. In other words, past performance records can be very helpful to do the job. But in intelligence analysis, such records are not available. Therefore, if one stays focused on simply trying to "manage uncertainties," there is a considerable risk that the analyst will try to force the issue by making subjective (even arbitrary) judgments in assigning weights. By contrast, a "managing analytic flaws" approach flags such forcing of the issue as a major flaw to be avoided. It strongly cautions against trying to assign specific weights when good performance records are missing. It helps analysts "manage" the problem by providing guidance on how to refine equal weighting, so it can serve as a prudent, albeit imperfect, work around (see also note 7).

16 In 2005, Professor Tetlock presented a heavily researched critique of the record of experts in making predictions in a wide variety of fields. (See Philip E. Tetlock, *Expert Political Judgment: How Good Is It? How Can We Know?* Princeton University Press, Princeton 2005.) In this work, Professor Tetlock emphasized the importance of "accountability"—of experts having to keep track of, and accept responsibility for, their predictions. (The lack of decent performance records over the years obviously complicates—and, for some, seemingly alleviates—this issue for intelligence analysts and their superiors. But inadequate records also mean that those who might claim responsibility for intelligence successes wind up having more missed opportunities for recognition, since the records particularly slight successes. Failures not successes, after all, have been the subject of big post mortems.) More recently, Professor Tetlock has been on a long term contract with the Intelligence Advanced Research Projects Activity (IARPA) to develop techniques for improving intelligence prediction. At least some of them are reflected in his recent best seller (with Dan Gardner), *Superforecasting: The Art and Science of Prediction*, Crown Publishers, New York, 2015.

17 Just as Tetlock's method and my own might usefully complement each other, I believe that other approaches to training intelligence analysts would also be best served by combining forces—rather than by being viewed as stark alternatives. This especially applies to a juxtaposition that is frequently made between expertise cultivated by scientific method and expertise gained by training in country or regional studies. (As a Sovietologist when I began my professional career, I came to appreciate early on that melding the two types of expertise was both feasible and prudent. See note 1.) Since experts on some foreign culture can often differ—which was commonplace for experts claiming to be able to "think Soviet" during the Cold War—it makes sense for them to use hypothesis testing to see whose particular take on a given country issue is best supported by data and reasoning. By the same token, scientific method, as exemplified in hypothesis testing, often needs to draw on country or regional expertise to keep some relevant hypotheses and data from being left out of consideration. This is particularly likely with hypotheses and data that reflect foreign behavior that, while sensible within its own cultural context, would seem <u>irrational</u> from a Western point of view and might therefore be dismissed as implausible. (Ironically, really irrational behavior—such as in extreme terrorist acts—is hardly likely to be ignored.) See also notes 8 and 15.

18 A real world comparative methodology test, such as I propose, would differ in various ways from other analytic competitions that the U.S. IC has held over the years. Perhaps the most famous one is the Team B exercise in the 1970s concerning the Soviet strategic outlook, which pitted outside national security scholars against intelligence professionals who drafted the annual NIEs on Soviet strategic forces. This competition did not resolve the issue—in large part because it was not set up in a real test format—and was quite controversial, especially given the exceptional importance of its subject matter, and no similar competition was held subsequently. Tetlock's "superforecasting" approach grew out of a much more recent series of competitions involving large groups of individuals, drawn from various walks of life, whose predictive skills were compared on a variety of issues of interest to the IC. A key objective for Tetlock, as noted, was to identify individuals who were particularly good at predicting—"superforecasters"—and to distill guidelines from their ways of thinking that could teach others to predict better (see note 13).

In the test I propose, since intelligence professionals actually have to make the predictions for policymakers, I believe they are the only test group that should be involved. And, obviously, they should have the appropriate clearances to be able to use whatever secrets collectors can provide on the issue to be tested. Further, real testing (not an inconclusive comparison, such as in the Team B exercise) should be conducted to determine whether structured (e.g., Heuer's and mine) vs. unstructured approaches (e.g., Tetlock's) work best for rank and file analysts—and how these methods compare to the group consensus approach.

Finally, as earlier discussed, it is important to conduct the comparative testing of methods, not in a classroom setting (which is always somewhat artificial compared to an analyst's real life environment. See note 10), but in a "live" decision making situation. This calls for the competing methods to make a predictive judgment that is intended for policymakers and thus result in real world consequences, which can later be used to see which method worked best. Key intelligence officials overseeing this drill would, of course, have to put forward some judgment for their policymaking audience at the time—unlike in some classroom exercise—before the jury came in on the competing methodologies. Presumably, these officials would opt for the group consensus answer, while knowing for sure that a post mortem on all the competing methodologies awaited.

19 Those who are skeptical about the suitability of computerized statistical probability analysis for intelligence analysts certainly can point to some big glitches in its civilian world applications. For example, the errors witnessed in the predictions of the outcome of the 2016 U.S. presidential election are well-known. After his impressive success in predicting the 2012 results (see Chapter 4, p. 80), the prominent prognosticator, Nate Silver, and many others (perhaps even more so) got it wrong in 2016. A more telling note of caution, regarding the application of civilian world modeling techniques to intelligence analysis, is that intelligence analysts would lack two big advantages that Mr Silver and others have had—while still making such glitches. Intelligence analysts could not: (1) draw on performance records; and (2) unlike predicting the outcomes of most sporting events and elections, be quite confident that the eventual winner is among the known participants in the competition. As earlier discussed, intelligence analysts cannot be sure that the hypotheses they are comparing in a given case actually include the correct hypothesis (see p. 9). That is one reason why I urge them to consider many hypotheses. Supporters of group consensus can hardly tout this difference with civilian world techniques to sustain their own approach. They are, to say the least, poorly qualified to argue that intelligence analysis has a special need to cover alternative outcomes.

In any case, no glitches, big or small, in predictions made in the civilian world seem likely to halt, or even seriously slow, the march of the digital age in eventually affecting intelligence analysts' lives. At a minimum, in seeking government contracts, companies with strong corporate interests in the tools of the digital age can be expected to vigorously press the case for using statistical probability analysis with sophisticated mathematical modeling. They are unlikely to simply focus on cyber threats and enhancing technical collection, and ignore this aspect of the intelligence business as a potential market. Trying to deflect the coming demands of the digital age on intelligence analysis therefore is unlikely to work. By contrast, prudently adjusting to these demands, as I outline in Chapter 4, seems feasible. This means trying to ensure that modeling techniques and the like are sensibly adapted to meet the special requirements of intelligence analysis. Otherwise, using these techniques could well bear out a skeptic's fears and make intelligence failures more—rather than less—likely in the future. Pursuing this objective is where the talents and energies of those with a stake in sound intelligence analysis should be concentrated.

20 As Deputy National Intelligence Officer for Warning, helping to oversee warning collection in the mid-1990s, I had first-hand knowledge that, when crises hit, intelligence organizations are forcefully reminded of their principal mission. On a day-to-day basis, intelligence analysts have to compete to get priority for relevant collection of the secrets they seek. In crisis situations, however, warning needs supersede all relevant collection tasking. Given my warning background, I made special efforts in my methodology to ensure that it would be responsive to time-sensitive situations while also providing solid analysis. As illustrated in the Chapter 3 case study, the methodology is structured in stages (zero-based review/ shared consistency test, then inconsistency test, and finally missing data test). As each of the first two stages is completed, interim judgments can be made to give policymakers a useful early heads up on the threat or other issue being assessed.

Bibliography

Allison, Graham T., *Essence of Decision: Explaining the Cuban Missile Crisis*, 1st ed., Little, Brown, Boston, MA, 1971.

Allison, Graham T. (with Philip Zelikow), *Essence of Decision: Explaining the Cuban Missile Crisis*, 2nd ed., Longman, New York, 1999.

Clarke, Richard (with R.P. Eddy), *Warnings: Finding Cassandras to Stop Catastrophes*, Harper Collins, New York, 2017.

Davies, Will, "All in a Flap: Beware Unknown Unknowns. Review of Nassim Taleb's *The Black Swan: The Impact of the Highly Improbable*," *Oxonian Review of Books*, Issue 6.3, June 2007.

Government Publishing Office, *Unclassified Version of the Report of the Commission on the Intelligence Capabilities of the United States Regarding Weapons of Mass Destruction*, March 31, 2005: www.gpo.gov/fdsys/pkg/GPO-WMD/pdf/GPO-WMD.pdf.

Heuer, Richards J., *Psychology of Intelligence Analysis*, Kindle ed., Center for the Study of Intelligence, Central Intelligence Agency, Washington, DC, 2016.

Jervis, Robert, *Why Intelligence Fails: Lessons from the Iranian Revolution and the Iraq War*, Cornell University Press, Ithaca, NY, 2010.

Kahneman, Daniel, *Thinking, Fast and Slow*, Farrar, Straus & Giroux, New York, 2011.

National Commission on Terrorist Attacks Upon the United States, *Report of the National Commission on Terrorist Attacks Upon the United States*, Final Report, July 22, 2004: www.9-11commission.gov/report/911Report.pdf.

Popper, Sir Karl, *Conjectures and Refutations: The Growth of Scientific Knowledge*, Routledge Classics, London, 2000.

Silver, Nate, *The Signal and the Noise: Why So Many Predictions Fail—But Some Don't*, Penguin Books, New York, 2012.

Spielmann, Karl, *The Intellectual Imperative: Hegel's Response to Kant*, Ph.D. Dissertation, Harvard University, Cambridge, MA, 1974.

Spielmann, Karl, *Analyzing Soviet Strategic Arms Decisions*, Westview Press, Boulder, CO, 1978.

Tetlock, Philip E., *Expert Political Judgment: How Good Is It? How Can We Know?* Princeton University Press, Princeton, 2005.

Tetlock, Philip E. (with Dan Gardner), *Superforecasting: The Art and Science of Prediction*, Crown Publishers, New York, 2015.

2 Strengthening intelligence threat analysis[1]

Will the U.S. have to deal with threats—from terrorists or state adversaries—only when it has solid evidence in hand to avert them? Of course not. Even the most determined collection efforts to obtain actionable intelligence, therefore, will not suffice to meet current threat needs. Threats will continue to occur when only more fragmented and diffuse evidence is available. And in such situations analysis will have the key role to play.

In fact, if and when another big post mortem is held on some threat that intelligence has failed to predict or otherwise misjudged, analysis is likely to be more in the spotlight than ever before. The reason is simple: in the aftermath of the September 11, 2001 (9/11) attacks and the failure to find weapons of mass destruction (WMD) in Iraq in 2003, other major means to "fix" the threat assessment problem have already received a lot of attention.

Although perhaps not yet quite exhausted, the corrective measures employed to improve intelligence over the past decade and more have included large infusions of new resources, big organizational shakeups, and dramatic upgrades in gathering information. Indeed, data collection has been spurred to push the envelope—to the point of raising a number of legal and political controversies.[2] Analysis, of course, was hardly ignored by these earlier post mortems and some changes resulted. But to argue that analysis has experienced a comparable impetus to push the envelope in doing all it can to meet current threat needs would be difficult. So that some future post mortem should single out analysis for special scrutiny and call for some big changes to be made would not be surprising.[3]

But what might and should these big changes in analysis be? At least one important area where new techniques might be applied that could strengthen analysis as a partner with collection in assessing and predicting current threats is addressed here. And, because they would operate in the realm of analysis, the use of such enhanced techniques would have the virtue of being much less likely than enhanced collection techniques to encounter significant legal and political controversies. Alternative analysis, which is employed when conventional wisdom needs a fresh look, is an area where enhanced techniques could be used to better deal with current threats.

Alternative analysis

A standing objective for intelligence has been to promote open-mindedness among analysts. This entails a willingness to challenge whatever dominant view emerges on a given intelligence issue. Intelligence has called these challenges by different names, but alternative analysis appropriately captures their essence. To determine a foreign target's most probable course of action, such analysis offers alternatives to the prevailing view or conventional wisdom, then tests all views to see which is best supported, and thus most likely to be correct.

An inconsistency test is probably the most important and familiar tool for rigorous alternative analysis. The use of an inconsistency test has been a staple of intelligence alternative analysis techniques for decades. Richards Heuer provided the classic treatment of the technique in his analysis of competing hypotheses (ACH) methodology.[4] The general approach involves comparing alternative views with various bodies of relevant data to see which view has the most or fewest inconsistencies, and thus has the weakest or strongest claim to validity. The approach draws on the principles of scientific inquiry articulated by the prominent analyst of scientific method Karl Popper.[5] Popper tried to simplify inquiry by basically focusing on a process of elimination to show which competing theories on an issue were improbable. He stressed that a theory's consistency with even a large body of data could not prove it was valid, since other theories could be compatible with the same evidence—and those that qualified would have an equal claim to be valid. Popper looked to inconsistencies as a better discriminator, and emphasized the importance of finding relevant data that do not fit particular theories. Theories with numerous inconsistencies would be less likely to be valid; those with few or none would be more likely to be valid. The inconsistency test as adapted by Heuer for intelligence purposes provides a means to sort out competing hypotheses (on a wide array of intelligence issues) and rank them as to their relative validity on a given issue.

Falling short of potential

Alternative analysis (or any other basic approach) used in the intelligence business necessarily faces a standard that is tougher than any by which it would be judged in an academic setting. Namely, irrespective of how much it may have been developed and refined, or endorsed by its author's colleagues, or taught to students, the key question has to be: but has it made a difference where it counts? More particularly, has it helped intelligence get it right on major threat issues?

Intelligence has long officially called for critical thinking that is "outside the box" including the endorsement of the use of alternative analysis efforts. Yet, whether for the failure to find WMD in Iraq, or the 9/11 attacks, or the 1991 collapse of the Soviet threat, or Iraq's 1990 invasion of Kuwait, or the 1979 fall of Iran's Shah, or even earlier lapses in threat prediction, whatever alternatives may have been raised to the prevailing views obviously did not forestall these surprises. Whether in these cases no alternatives were advanced, or they were advanced but failed to make an impact, or they made an impact but were themselves seriously flawed, is of little matter. The result was the same—erroneous views ultimately prevailed. The upshot is that this record clearly bodes ill for the likelihood of alternative analysis having significant impact in forestalling surprises on some new major threat in the future.[6]

Shortcomings in the historical and ongoing treatment of alternative views are also seen in the Intelligence Community's (IC) estimative process. The practice of individual agencies registering a dissent in national estimates by taking a "footnote" that differs in some way from the mainstream view on an issue is long standing. That dissent, an alternative view, is normally accompanied by a citation of evidence to argue the case. In more recent years, this practice of putting forward alternative views has been essentially carried over to other publications. It has been given fresh impetus—along with some laudable institutional efforts such as the establishment of an analytic quality component in the Office of the Director of National Intelligence (DNI[7])—since the 9/11 and Iraq WMD surprises. "Red cell" reports or similar venues have been provided for IC analysts to air alternatives to mainstream views and present evidence to argue why intelligence and policy audiences should consider them.[8]

While appreciating that this basic practice of offering alternatives has inherent limitations, the practice can perform a useful service not only in promoting open-mindedness in the inter-agency estimate process but more generally in intelligence. The limitations, however, are that in presenting the alternatives—and even providing some evidence to back them up—what are being offered are essentially embryonic challenges to dominant views. They are only the first important step in trying to get it right, and not the culmination of a systematic process to do so. As such, the recipient winds up having to live with both the dominant view and the alternative view, without having adequate grounds to decide which of these views (or some other view) is more likely to be correct.

In short, alternative views, where presented, are usually not carried forward to a conclusive contest with the dominant view they purport to challenge. Rather, they are simply allowed to stand and audiences can mistakenly come to believe they are either more, or perhaps less, significant than they really are. Historically, the IC's Team A/Team B clash in the 1970s on Soviet strategic objectives[9] and perhaps a few other cases might argue that serious contests have occurred—but, if so, in the overall estimate record they still would be rarities. (To test for any sustained community promotion of alternative views, analysts could look into this record for examples of an alternative view actually supplanting an original mainstream view. The absence of such examples would suggest a lack of real contests or that, if and when any such contests occurred, alternatives never emerged as winners.)

Accepting the conventional wisdom

Absent a conclusive contest on some issue, intelligence and policy audiences are merely being asked to accept that the mainstream view and the alternative view (or views) can somehow just coexist. That this would have a certain appeal in an estimate setting is understandable since it seems sound bureaucratically. Such coexistence enables collective judgments to be made while allowing individual agencies a chance to express their autonomy. But, in terms of giving policymakers the best guidance on what is likely the truth (presumably the main purpose of an assessment), this practice does not pass a basic test of logic—that is, since only one real world exists out there, the mainstream view and the alternative(s) obviously cannot both be right about that reality. Without waiting for history's verdict or obtaining compelling evidence, only one way is available to find out whether the dominant view or some alternative view is closer to the truth: subjecting the different views to a testing process—one which provides some means to rank them—to see how each holds up when all pertinent evidence is taken into account.

If rigorous impartial testing of both dominant views and their alternatives is not carried out, assessments can be less than helpful to consumers in various ways. At best, the issue at hand can seem more uncertain than it really needs to be—the failure to sort out which is the better or best view can merely reinforce the oft-heard lament that intelligence provides a lot of "on the one hand/on the other hand" judgments. More serious perhaps is that the dominant view can simply win by default. For that dominant view, in an estimate setting, after all enjoys the winning votes from agency representatives. But such votes per se are not a sound basis for making a call, although they may seem impressive to some IC consumers. The question persists: how can they be sound, if a thorough and explicit weighing of the evidence and reasoning behind both the dominant view and its challengers has not been made? And, moreover, how can key consumers knowledgeably judge which view they should believe, if such testing has not been done and then communicated clearly to them?

In sum, alternative analysis lacks a good track record in helping to forestall surprises on major threat issues. Its potential has also not been realized in national estimates or "red cell" reports, where it has basically stopped short of a serious process of testing, despite the fact that alternative analysis methodologies that call for such testing have long been on the books.

Enhanced analytic techniques

To better meet current threat needs, alternative analysis should be both as rigorous as possible and taken more seriously. Various ways may help make this happen, but the use of four new techniques would be a good start. Each technique can individually benefit analysis. And, when used together, they can constitute a coherent process of testing. Such a process can strengthen collective judgments on the probability of a given threat, which particularly matters when threats can have potentially severe consequences.

The recommended measures to enhance alternative analysis are:

Technique one: prudently stretch analytic imagination by testing many hypotheses.

Technique two: independently check source vetting to better detect deception.

Technique three: systematically assess missing data to better determine validity and detect foreign denial.

Technique four: make a common sense start with a zero-based review of a dominant view's evidence and reasoning.

Technique one: prudently stretch analytic imagination by testing many hypotheses

One special need is to ensure no available data of importance for identifying and assessing a potential threat are overlooked. Since 9/11 "connecting the dots" has been the popular catch phrase for identifying and relating pertinent evidence on threats.[10] "Connecting the dots," however, often calls for more than better sharing of information among intelligence organizations—the understandable focus of concern in the major bureaucratic realignments over the past decade and more. Also important is the matter of how to actually think about the threat problem. Are the dots expected to be blatant enough that they will guide analysts' thinking to be able to make the right connections? Or must an analyst be imaginative enough to come up with the right concepts for looking at data so that the "dots" that matter can be appreciated? One indicator of how difficult these basic issues of sorting out the relationship between concepts and evidence can be is that, in one form or another, these issues have bedeviled major philosophers for centuries.[11]

An analytic approach can hardly solve the problem of putting the right bureaucratic ducks in order, but it can help deal with the way analysts think about the threat problem. In particular, relying solely on the single lens of a dominant view can cause certain important "dots" to go unnoticed in the first place, especially when they are immersed in a sea of raw data. To help bring such important data to light, the use of many hypotheses would therefore seem sensible. This could be done in a new inconsistency test that would be an adaptation of Richards Heuer's ACH methodology.

The new enhanced analytic technique would essentially combine two practices that on their own are not novel. First, terrorist threat analysts have been regularly enjoined to consider a broad array of threat possibilities. Second, alternative analysis methodologies such as Heuer's ACH have, over the years, regularly provided for the generation and formal testing of hypotheses. These practices would simply be melded in a new inconsistency test. In contrast to the normal procedure in alternative analysis methodologies of using perhaps three to four hypotheses, using more—even considerably more—hypotheses would be called for. What, in earlier years, might have been a somewhat cumbersome chore of manipulating a large number of hypotheses and associated data sets can now be greatly facilitated by appropriate software. In any event, the use of many hypotheses can help directly address—in a structured and systematic fashion—the concern voiced by the National Commission on Terrorist Attacks Upon the United States (the 9/11 Commission) for analysts to have greater imagination in considering the kinds of threats terrorists might attempt.[12] Further, using many hypotheses also can help make other enhanced analytic techniques work.

The beneficial use of multiple hypotheses gives analysts an opportunity to include one or more that explicitly provide explanations for or insight into unique or unexpected foreign behavior. Otherwise, such hypotheses might often not make the cut for testing, basically because they might seem "irrational" by U.S. standards. Although some irrational behavior by adversaries, such as suicide attacks, would doubtless make the cut, being wary of simply planning to fight the last war is always prudent. Useful to remember is that the kinds of attacks that now tend to drive perceptions of the terrorist threat got scant attention prior to 9/11. The inclusion of hypotheses that focus explicitly on unique or unexpected adversary behavior can help analysts better deal with various situational factors affecting a target's actions—such as special political, cultural, and religious constraints and, for a target's military capability, even possible home grown approaches to solve technical problems.

Even if using many hypotheses yielded no other benefits, it would still be important for one overriding reason: it provides multiple lenses on reality that bring important data into an analyst's field of vision—data that normally would not be so brought by the single lens of a dominant view. This is not just a matter of having more data to notice. It is also because those using different hypotheses on a threat (or other issue) will, by their nature, be on the lookout for certain data that are particularly relevant to support their case. To illustrate how this natural focus of a hypothesis on finding supporting data can really matter, a body of data made famous by the 9/11 Commission as having been underappreciated prior to the attacks—data indicating suspicious flight training[13]—should be considered. Leaving aside the pros and cons of the Commission's specific treatment of this issue, supposing for sake of argument that a dominant view prevailing at the time on how terrorists would strike at the U.S. did not feature a suicide attack with a commercial airplane. Suppose, also for sake of argument, that an alternative hypothesis did feature such an attack. Which hypothesis would be more likely to prompt analysts to look for data indicating suspicious flight training? The answer would seem obvious.

Moreover, for those believing that only a few hypotheses—as opposed to many—might be all that is needed to call attention to key data, further consideration should be given to the fact that threat scenarios generally have a number of variables or key questions for analysts to address. For example, if an alternative hypothesis called attention to data on "suspicious flight training," it would be bringing to light information that addresses the variable of what an attack could entail—specifically, the use of a commercial airplane for a suicide mission. But, even assuming the flight training data further reveal who is receiving the training, assessing the potential attack should also include the variables to consider of when, where, and how (e.g., various strike options for using planes) the attack might happen. And these variables could matter for ultimately getting a handle on the big variable of whether an attack was likely—that is, determining its probability. Hypotheses could differ in various ways not only on what kind of attack might take place (and by whom) but on each of the pertinent questions of when, where, and how. In so doing, they would likely call attention to certain bodies or items of data to support their contentions that their competitors might overlook. In short, using only a couple or even a few hypotheses would be unlikely to adequately exploit the fertile ground for bringing key data to light that a typical threat scenario might offer.

Caution is important, however, when databases contain masses of essentially raw data—as might be case with some terrorist threat databases that pull together information from various contributors—that the use of many hypotheses can hardly be expected on its own to provide all the insights needed to identify and predict a specific threat. Establishing the potential relevance of such data to any particular threat would generally require considerable work involving inputs from various fields of expertise to filter the information. Again, the example of "suspicious flight training" data offers a useful perspective. As noted, a given hypothesis will prompt analysts to be on the lookout for bodies or items of data that are particularly relevant to support the view posited by the hypothesis. And, in the case of "suspicious flight training" data, a hypothesis that posits the threat to be a suicide attack using a commercial airplane could well find such data to be particularly relevant. But for there to be "suspicious flight training" data in the first place— that can be used to see how this view of the threat holds up against its rivals—someone at some level must in effect provide the initial filter that identifies certain flight training data as "suspicious."

As for overall data handling, the use of many hypotheses may require analysts to juggle more information than many methodologies—using fewer hypotheses—have tended to call for. Even so, modern computer applications should be able to facilitate the required data handling. A software version of Heuer's ACH methodology, for example, already exists. Also, analysts working on assessing terrorist threats routinely draw on numerous large-scale computerized databases to assemble, correlate, and winnow information from law enforcement and other contributors to try to identify and track potential threats. The use of many hypotheses would be an additional, but perhaps sometimes crucial, tool that could be applied to these databases to help sort the data. Moreover, "using many hypotheses" would be much more than just generating many hypotheses to bring key data to light. That alone would not be much of an advance on the usual practice of laying out an array of threat possibilities for analysts to consider.[14] For analysts really to benefit, testing of these hypotheses must take place. And this can be done by determining which hypothesis has the fewest inconsistencies with data already identified as relevant and important.

Technique two: independently check source vetting to better detect deception

Another special need is to more thoroughly assess source reliability. When time and circumstances permit, analysis can contribute more here than generally believed, so that interrogation need not do this often difficult job alone. After all, the potential consequences of an undetected deception hardly need mention. Vetting results, including for technical sources, can be incorporated in the new inconsistency test adapted from Heuer's ACH methodology and a comparison can then be made with other data to check these results.

An enhanced analytic technique to independently check source reliability could proceed as follows:

1 Incorporate as a separate data set in the inconsistency test the vetting results on the source of the insider information. Vetting is a routine requirement for human sources and normally involves a polygraph exam. But technically acquired information is not per se immune to compromise—and compromise could result in the technical source being used to convey deceptive information. Vetting, therefore, is also pertinent for technical sources. It would entail a risk assessment by the relevant technical collectors of the chances for compromise, which, certainly for high impact issues, they should be urged to undertake. (Such assessments at least have been occasionally done but merit more regular use on threat issues.) But vetting of either human or technical sources cannot be assumed to be infallible in detecting deception. Hence, it is important to double-check.

2 Compare the view supported by the insider evidence with all of the evidence that has been assembled to test this view and its competitors for inconsistencies. By definition, the insider information itself, as well as favorable vetting results on the source, would be consistent with the view in question. The key issue, however, is how this view holds up against other data in the test. If the view supported by the insider information has few or no inconsistencies with other data, this would show that the insider information is probably sound, and a favorable vetting result on that source is probably reliable. Obviously, if an inconsistency check were run to see if unfavorable vetting results were warranted on a source, few or no inconsistencies would cast doubt on this vetting.

3 Be mindful of a potential pitfall. What if the foreign target were able to manipulate other data to lend credence to the information from the insider source? The view in question would then lack inconsistencies

with these data as well, and could thus appear to have a stronger claim to be valid than was really the case. Since foreign targets would naturally have incentives to manipulate other data to achieve this result, still other measures are needed to help ensure the integrity of the inconsistency check on vetting. Having numerous diverse data becomes highly important. For a foreign target to manipulate multiple, diverse data would be difficult. And a similar precaution makes sense when dealing with missing data to check whether foreign denial is at work. The basic principle for detecting deception or denial is this: the more numerous and diverse the relevant data, the less likely the view in question (in the inconsistency test) is a deception or (in the missing data test) a victim of denial. And this in turn further argues for using many hypotheses to bring to attention as much relevant data as possible.

To detect a personal fabrication, only a small number of alternative data sources to use as a check on the vetting might suffice. A source who was not acting as an agent of a foreign target would not normally be in a position to manipulate various sources of data to lend credence to his or her lies. But to ensure a source was neither a personal fabricator nor an agent perpetrating a deception, multiple, diverse data would be called for.

Even using numerous and diverse data for an inconsistency test check on deception, ensuring that the inconsistency test check works off a prior vetting effort (which, at least for human sources, will likely have been done anyway) is still prudent. In other words, having two checks on a potential deception is advisable. Using multiple, diverse data as a gauge can indicate whether a deception is less likely, but doing so cannot guarantee that a sophisticated deception will be unable to slip through the cracks. For example, in World War II, the Allies helped make the D-Day landing successful, because they flummoxed Nazi Germany with a multi-pronged deception involving various sources of information on which Germany was relying.[15] Even if rare, complex deceptions can still happen.

Another important aspect of solving the deception problem is that the context which an inconsistency test provides for assessing hypotheses should be ideally suited for ensuring the detection of a deception can be fully exploited. The basic objective of dealing with deception is not just to find out what is not the truth. Rather, it is to help find out what is the truth—and this cannot be accomplished by merely staying focused on the deception alone. The deception must be viewed in a broader context—and an inconsistency test, by its nature, meets this need. It places the deception in the context of other views that offer different interpretations of the foreign target's course of action. One of those views will probably be the truth. In effect, an inconsistency test—followed by a missing data test— provides a structured means to link up deception with denial. A foreign target providing phony information to make an incorrect view seem valid is also likely to be trying to deny information that would help validate the correct view. Thus once deception is detected for one view in the inconsistency test, analysts should expect some other view to be a victim of denial which a missing data test can then assess.

Technique three: systematically assess missing data to better determine validity and detect foreign denial

A further need is to deal systematically with missing data as a factor affecting the validity of alternative views, given the greater unknowns to be faced about modern adversaries. On its own, an inconsistency test cannot adequately judge the relative validity of contending views—no matter how rigorous and comprehensive it may be—because the potential impact of missing data is not included. To fill that gap and to accompany the inconsistency test on available data, a missing data test can be devised, duly taking into account inevitable uncertainties in such an endeavor. The aim of the test is to determine, in regard to the hypotheses examined in the inconsistency test, how many items or bodies of critical data each might be missing, in addition to whatever inconsistencies they might have been assessed to include. As with inconsistencies, hypotheses should hope to have little or no missing data. When the missing data are tallied, hypotheses can be ranked in terms of the combined total of inconsistencies and missing data each has. The hypothesis with the lowest combined number would have the strongest overall claim to be correct; the one with the highest number would have the weakest claim.

When analysts employ a missing data test many refinements would doubtless need to be made. For example, military issues, political issues, economic issues, and the like have certain data types unique to each. A hypothesis on some military issue should not be faulted for lacking polling data to back up its case. Yet this could be a perfectly reasonable requirement if a political issue were involved. That a missing data test in all cases would not ignore the impact of missing data in making an evaluation of the strengths and weaknesses of a given hypothesis is its basic virtue. And it would be more systematic and impartial than simply judging a hypothesis in isolation in terms of the key data it might be missing. Most analysts, for example, would be well aware if a hypothesis lacked corroborating evidence to support certain direct evidence on which it was relying. But how detrimental that might be should not be judged in a vacuum. Would it not matter if competing views could cite no direct evidence at all in making their cases? A missing data test would deal with these sorts of comparative considerations.

Once an inconsistency test has been done, a missing data test should not be all that difficult to set up. It basically involves taking the competing hypotheses on a given intelligence issue and arraying them against a checklist of generic types of data that are relevant for that issue, as suggested by the claims and extant support each hypothesis has brought to the table in the inconsistency test. Moreover, for a given topic area, an analyst's checklist might cover not only basic generic types of data—such as documentary evidence, observational data, and the like—but also, as appropriate, specific categories of sensitive sources that may be relevant to the issue.

Key considerations for identifying the most significant types of missing data for individual hypotheses might include:

- A situation in which one hypothesis has direct evidence from an insider source to support it and the other views do not. Obviously, this would be difficult for other views to counter unless they too could secure such direct evidence in their behalf.
- Also, a number of hypotheses could posit the existence of various capabilities and thus have an evident need to establish this. Important missing data therefore might be observational data from imagery or technical information that feasibility assessments could provide—information indicating whether these capabilities reasonably could exist.

The inconsistency test also can provide insights for an analyst to determine the appropriate priority for seeking missing data. They can help identify data that should be sought currently and therefore can be deemed critical needs and data that may be needed in the future. For example:

- Hypothesis X may be supported by direct evidence and may have had that evidence both favorably vetted and favorably checked by the inconsistency test. And this hypothesis might also face competitors lacking any direct evidence to support their view. Under these circumstances, the first priority would be for the competitors to come up with such evidence. Securing further corroboration for X's direct evidence would be less critical but could be a future missing data task.

The Missing Data Conundrum. A key reason for why methodologies probably have steered clear of dealing with missing data is that it inevitably involves coping with seemingly daunting uncertainties. The missing data test must deal with these uncertainties as well. In fact, using many hypotheses (which both the inconsistency and missing data tests feature) can help reduce—albeit not eliminate—these uncertainties and other measures also can help. Probably the biggest uncertainty is that, since "you don't know what you don't know," an analyst may not be aware that some missing data could actually exist. Whether or not a target is actively denying these data to U.S. collection, as discussed below, the main problem is that the U.S. might not even be looking for the information. This uncertainty underscores the importance of using many hypotheses to broaden an analyst's awareness. It also makes securing direct insider information particularly necessary. It is the data source most likely to bring such unknowns to light and thus identify them for further collection. Feasibility assessments also can help, for example, by pointing to capabilities that potentially could exist.

Just as an inconsistency test needs to deal with the issue of whether certain available data are deceptive, a missing data test must deal with the denial issue because it directly affects how missing data can be interpreted. Specifically, do data that collectors are unable to find ultimately suggest a particular hypothesis may be invalid or can they suggest instead that it may be valid? A missing data test can help guide data searches but provides no guarantees missing data will be found. Since most competing hypotheses will be invalid, by definition their important supporting data should be missing and stay missing. But a valid hypothesis may also be unable to secure certain key data it might be missing as a result of adversary denial efforts.[16] After all, a valid hypothesis is the truth that a target does not want U.S. intelligence to know. As a result, the U.S. will be in a contest in which the target's active opposition, using denial and deception (D&D), may be able to frustrate even a determined data search.

A well-known expression neatly sums up this uncertainty of whether missing data indicate whether a hypothesis is invalid or point to a valid hypothesis for which supporting data are being denied: "Absence of evidence is not (necessarily) evidence of absence."[17] For example, the inability to find data confirming a suspected foreign military capability does not necessarily mean the data and thus the capability do not exist. The array of D&D measures that a target can use compounds the problem. Analysts cannot even assume that discovering indications of D&D activity itself provides a good clue as to where the truth lies—which would, on its own, help make the case that a given hypothesis is valid. Thus, detecting denial measures—such as a security perimeter—at some facility might seem a sure sign that the target has something to hide there. But these measures could be deceptive, intended for the U.S. to detect but really to throw it off the track of the real secret.

Consequently, if a given view is treated in isolation, as has usually been the case in the IC's treatment of D&D issues, it can be difficult to determine whether—even with a vigorous collection effort—key data to support it remain missing because the hypothesis is: (a) invalid or (b) valid but victimized by D&D. Because of their comparative context of using many hypotheses, however, the inconsistency and missing data tests together provide two checks that reduce this uncertainty. First, the inconsistency test results provide preliminary judgments on the likely validity of a hypothesis. The missing data test's comparison of the various data each hypothesis is missing provides a second check. Targets might well be capable of keeping the truth hidden if they can focus denial efforts on one or even a few different sources of information. Yet, if more than a few data sources are involved and they are diverse, denial is less likely to be at work. As noted earlier, deception is also subject to two checks—the original vetting and then the check to see if a target would have to provide multiple, diverse (bogus) data to pull it off. Thus, if a hypothesis both fares poorly in the inconsistency test and cannot find a number of diverse missing data, it is probably not being denied the data but is simply invalid. And the converse would apply.

Technique four: make a common sense start with a zero-based review of a dominant view's evidence and reasoning

Intelligence analysis necessarily takes place in a bureaucratic setting that affects the pursuit and dissemination of the truth. Bureaucracies are inherently conservative, according to social scientists who have studied them,[18] and the insufficient impact of alternative analysis over the years suggests intelligence bureaucracies are no exception. Such conservatism, in fact, is to be expected. Dominant views in intelligence analysis would not truly be dominant unless key officials at various levels in these bureaucracies, not just analysts, bought into them. Some officials may even stake their reputations on them. Consequently, new or different views can have many minds to change and strong vested interests to overcome. Therefore, if the basic bureaucratic set up of intelligence gives officials incentives to be wary of embracing alternative views, significant institutional adjustments may ultimately be necessary to encourage them to be more receptive. For now, these officials might be engaged by urging zero-based reviews, to make clear to them whether a dominant view has weaknesses they may not have appreciated.

By definition, a dominant view represents a standing claim to be the correct view on some intelligence issue. Consequently, whether or not other views eventually come into play, the dominant view's proponents have a common sense, bedrock requirement to back up this claim by justifying it with appropriate evidence and sound reasoning. They should be prepared to show, for example, whether or not key data are recent or could be dated; whether direct or circumstantial evidence provides the main support; and what the underlying assumptions are, along with any other pertinent features of their evidence and reasoning. In effect, they would be providing a zero-based review to make clear why the dominant view should be believed. With the expectation that analysts have both assembled the relevant evidence and thought about it seriously before offering the view in the first place, providing such a demonstration of a dominant view's underpinnings should not be difficult—merely routine.

To be most useful, however, the zero-based review should be very explicit in identifying both the strengths and weaknesses supporting a given dominant view. And here analysts may particularly need to draw on methodological insights to identify any key weaknesses in their underlying assumptions. (Such weaknesses have been a favorite topic of many methodologies, which focus on trying to counter analytic cognitive biases.[19]) Even so, a potential key weakness in a dominant view's basic assumptions that existing methodologies have not made a focus of concern involves mistakenly assuming that certain key data are consistent with the dominant view alone. Failure to address this potential weakness can have substantial consequences, as demonstrated in the case of Iraqi WMD. More generally, it can affect the chances for key officials in the intelligence bureaucracies to take alternative analysis seriously in assessing any threats.

A subtle but critical need, if alternative analysis is to be heeded by key bureaucratic officials, is to buttress an inconsistency test so that dominant views do not have an undeserved edge in competing with other views. For example, a dominant view could rest its claim to be the correct view going into the test on the assertion that it is consistent with, and thus supported by, an impressive body of data. If this assertion is simply allowed to stand, a dominant view could still seem relatively strong even if the test shows it to have some inconsistencies with other data. One consequence is that analysts and their superiors who have backed the dominant view are unlikely to be persuaded to sign on to some new view. But merely claiming consistency is not a sound basis for a hypothesis to assert its validity. This assertion only holds up if the hypothesis can show that it alone is consistent with the relevant data. Thus, prior to an inconsistency test, a new zero-based review of a dominant view's support is called for, particularly to assess consistency claims.

Analysts have been regularly cautioned about relying on consistency (those using Heuer's ACH methodology will certainly have been warned), but having a clear appreciation of why it is a bad idea to do so is also essential. If different views share consistency on a given body of data, logically each would have an equal claim to validity based on that data. For most analysts, to be as concerned about the danger of shared consistency as the danger of making an argument inconsistent with key evidence may seem counterintuitive. But real world examples suggest that it is critical for analysts to avoid having, in effect, a misplaced confidence in the consistency of their view with key data. Rather, they need to ask whether this evidence could be consistent with other views—especially when they have worked an issue for a long time and have thus gotten comfortable with the data supporting their view.

The Allies' failure to find WMD in Iraq may be particularly instructive.[20] For this discussion, the precise reasons why Saddam changed course so that U.S. intelligence failed in 2003 to find WMD as expected are not the key issue. What matters is that, certainly by 2003, at least a significant body of evidence that analysts were continuing to see must have also been consistent with a quite different interpretation of Saddam. Otherwise, major inconsistencies would have been registered that called into question the prevailing intelligence view. A plausible interpretation of how this could have happened is that Saddam, knowing his WMD program was under close scrutiny and wanting to avoid tipping his hand that he had changed tack (for whatever reason), would have had strong incentives to keep U.S. intelligence seeing pretty much what it had gotten used to seeing. Thus, certainly by 2003, key data could well have been consistent with at least two different views: (1) Iraq was maintaining its WMD efforts as expected; and (2) Iraq was not maintaining them but wanted, at a minimum, to still keep U.S. intelligence guessing. But both views could not have been correct. Unfortunately, only unprecedented access to Iraq's WMD status once Gulf War II got under way, not analytic inquiry before the fact, showed the first view was wrong.

How significant can shared consistency be then for a dominant view's claims to be correct on some issue—particularly for a dominant view that relies heavily on a particular body of data? Simple math shows that—instead of still having a "pretty good" claim to be correct—the dominant view's claim would be undermined. If one other view qualifies as being consistent, the dominant view's odds of being correct based on the body of data can only be 1 in 2 (i.e., a 50 percent probability). If two or three other views qualify, the odds drop to 1 in 3 and 1 in 4 respectively, and worsen even further if more views qualify. The basic lesson: when consistency with a body of data is shared, the support the data provide for a given view cannot be strong; it can only be weak or very weak.

The significance of shared consistency makes important the holding of a dominant view to account before an inconsistency test is held. If a dominant view seems to be supported by an impressive body of data despite being shown to have some inconsistencies with other data, its backers will not only be reluctant to give it up. Methodologically, any competing views would also be faced with an unfair task in the inconsistency test. The working assumption would be that they are inconsistent with the supporting evidence brought to the test by the dominant view. They would then either have to live with this inconsistency, which would make them seem weaker than they really are, or be obliged to refute it. But they should not bear this onus. The dominant view's task is to show that its consistency with its key body of supporting data is exclusive—and to do so before facing specific competitors. Otherwise, its standing claim to be the correct view is simply specious.

Sharing consistency. But how can proponents of a dominant view meet this challenge? They can do so by carrying out a shared consistency test. This test would not be intended to stand alone but rather would be an integral part of a zero-based review of a dominant view's overall strengths and weaknesses. As a new test for analysts, however, it would represent the basis of what can be dubbed a new zero-based review. Specifically aimed at helping analysts avoid having a misplaced confidence in consistency, on a given threat issue the test would call for analysts to carefully examine whether any plausible circumstances might make other views consistent with the dominant view's key evidence. Such an assessment might show convincingly that no plausible circumstances exist. Or it might be unable to make a convincing case. Presumably, as analysts use this test on various threat issues, they would see the need to refine the basic question about shared consistency. One essential refinement, suggested by Saddam's behavior, would be for analysts to focus particularly on whether there are circumstances in which a view consistent with the dominant view's key evidence, but entailing "irrational" adversary behavior, merits serious consideration.[21] In general, a dominant view is ultimately not alone in facing the challenge of shared consistency. In competing in an inconsistency test, a number of views are likely to share consistency on various bodies of data. But, to win, one view alone must be consistent—and its competitors inconsistent—with certain bodies of data.

The payoff of subjecting a dominant view, at the outset, to a new zero-based review of its evidence and reasoning is that an inconsistency test and its outcome are more likely to matter, particularly to key officials in intelligence bureaucracies. The review gives alternative views a better chance to compete on a level playing field in an inconsistency test. As a result, one of them may actually wind up supplanting a dominant view rather than becoming, at best, just a caveat appended to it. Also, the new zero-based review can help convince skeptics why one should even bother to conduct an inconsistency test in the first place. If a dominant view cannot make a case that it alone is consistent with its main supporting evidence, that any other views that might share this consistency should be given a serious hearing should be obvious. An inconsistency test is well suited to bringing additional evidence to bear to sort out competing hypotheses.

Box 2.1 "Compelling evidence": an exemption from the new alternative analysis tests

Sometimes intelligence may be able to obtain "compelling evidence" on some issue—which some might refer to as real "smoking gun" or "slam dunk" quality evidence. By whatever name, it is evidence deemed to be of sufficient quality to make the testing using the four techniques much less necessary. This could matter when rapid decisions are required to avert a threat, which could outweigh gaining any added assurance of accuracy from such testing.

No precise definition of compelling evidence is possible and in the main it would be compelling in the eyes of expert beholders: a person with relevant expertise will know it when seeing it. For example, compelling evidence might be critical information about some imminent threat from a well-established insider human source, who: (a) is clearly in a position to know about the threat; (b) has been accurate in prior reporting; and (c) is not contradicted by other extant information relevant to the threat. Technical information with like credentials would also qualify as compelling.

More generally, compelling evidence would be so evidently complete and well-established when collected that it could basically stand on its own, requiring little or no analysis of any sort to convince intelligence professionals and their national security customers to heed it. "Connecting the dots" is then mainly a collection and sharing problem. If professionals have some uncertainty about whether the evidence they have obtained qualifies as compelling, an obvious litmus test is available: see if it convinces known responsible skeptics. If for good reasons they are not convinced and the issue does not require an immediate response, the evidence is not compelling enough to be exempted from the new alternative analysis testing.

Putting the techniques together: a coherent process to assess and predict threats

Since the new techniques will take considerable effort to implement, the only question that matters is: are they worth it? Partly, this will depend on an answer no methodology can provide. Intelligence professionals and their national security customers must decide whether the issues they face carry severe costs for intelligence failure. Presumably, they would appreciate that various terrorist and other threats merit special efforts to reduce the chances for error.

Partly, the answer will depend on whether the proposed enhanced techniques for alternative analysis, compared to other available approaches, can best assess conventional wisdom on such high impact issues. These techniques can be flexibly employed as follows:

1   If the objective is a scrub of the dominant view on an issue to see if has some major weaknesses, the proposed zero-based review of its data support and reasoning would meet this need. But various extant methodologies also aim to identify a number of the key weaknesses that a zero-based review would look for (for a sample, see Jack Davis discussion in Internet entries under Heuer[22]). The proposed zero-based review, however, focuses on identifying a serious potential weakness that other methodologies are less likely to emphasize, that is, the dominant view's main supporting data, such as key evidence on Iraqi WMD prior to Gulf War II,[23] may also be consistent with other views.

2   If the objective is also to find out whether better explanations than the dominant view might be available, the proposed inconsistency test can do this job, but it is hardly the first test that seeks to assess inconsistencies. In contrast, the new inconsistency test emphasizes using more hypotheses than a standard test to help ensure that no relevant available data of importance (such as suspicious flight training data prior to 9/11[24]) are slighted or ignored and more thoroughly checks source reliability.

3   If the objective is a ranking of all the competing hypotheses, the proposed new test on missing data complements the new inconsistency test by systematically treating missing data, which enables the making of a credible overall ranking. Moreover, this ranking can be presented numerically, which provides greater precision and clarity than using terms such as "possible," "probable," or "highly likely" to describe individual hypotheses. The ranking would simply combine the results of both tests, toting up the inconsistencies that each hypothesis has been assessed (and obliged to try to refute) and the number of key missing data it needs to secure.[25] The hypothesis with the fewest overall "validation tasks" would thus qualify as the strongest view— that is, the view that is most likely to be correct. By contrast, a standard inconsistency test alone can provide only a preliminary ranking, since it omits giving any systematic treatment of missing data needs for each hypothesis.

The proposed enhanced analytic techniques, therefore, provide options for meeting various requirements for conducting alternative analysis while offering additional help beyond what existing methodologies already afford analysts. Furthermore, key national security customers do not have to wait for all three tests to be completed in order to have useful (interim) intelligence judgments for any policy or military deliberations that may be under way on the threat issue at stake. Indeed, when time is truly of the essence, the zero-based review alone can provide valuable insights for these intelligence consumers. By its nature, the dominant view should have its support readily at hand to be scrutinized for potential weaknesses.

In one way or another, the problem areas that the proposed techniques address will have to be dealt with by analysis for two key reasons: (1) collection alone cannot meet current threat needs; and (2) the problem areas the techniques address can keep analysis from effectively helping out if they are simply slighted or ignored. Far from being on the periphery of intelligence analysis, these problem areas are knotty issues at its core, certainly in dealing with threats. Important available data can easily be overlooked. Vetting is not infallible in detecting deception. Even given their attendant uncertainties, missing data do matter and need serious treatment, if only to better determine denial. Dominant views likewise need scrubbing to pinpoint weaknesses, including a misplaced confidence in consistency. In addition, these problem areas have persisted for a long time, despite numerous cycles of intelligence failures and the lessons learned from them. Although some might maintain that a number of these problem areas have gotten adequate attention over the years, the 9/11 and Iraqi WMD cases alone argue that at best better remedies could only have been put in place very recently. And whether even now appropriate fixes are already in place for all of them is highly doubtful.[26]

The technique proposed here for a given problem area is not necessarily the only potential remedy and analysts and other methodologists should weigh in with their own. Indeed, some of these problems, such as not overlooking key available data on terrorist threats, are so difficult that no potentially valuable contribution to deal with them should be slighted. Beyond the help they might provide on individual problem areas, however, the techniques proposed herein have been devised so that they complement and reinforce each other and do not require disparate approaches to be somehow cobbled together to cover the full spectrum of problems.

The strongest selling point for using the techniques is that they can be presented together in a structured coherent process—first the proposed zero-based review, then the inconsistency test, and finally the missing data test. When the process is fully carried out, it can help the IC meet its unavoidable core responsibility to determine probability, particularly in predicting threats, when, as frequently happens, compelling evidence is unobtainable.

Box 2.2 A bureaucratic measure to help implement the techniques

The enhanced analytic techniques to bolster alternative analysis are unlikely to avoid contention, since there will be various personal and institutional stakeholders in the issues they examine. One measure to help convince all concerned that such techniques are at least rigorous and impartial would be to engage outside experts, particularly on high impact issues, not as an alternate team to in-house professionals but as a review panel. At a minimum, getting the testing process proposed herein—or a similar one—accepted as a legitimate norm for assessing high impact issues by engaging such panels would help defang the problem of real or alleged politicization, which these issues can invite because of their importance. Whether favored or disfavored by powerful interested parties, no view on an adversary's behavior would get a pass and would have to prove itself in a tough and fair competition to determine which view has the strongest claim to validity.

These panels would be intended to function, in effect, as a modest version of the prominent commissions that do post mortems. But, in contrast to the big commissions that are instituted after a catastrophe and then disbanded once their recommendations have been made, these panels would be an on-call resource to be tapped by analysts as evolving threat needs warrant. Their key mission would be to help analysts detect and correct errors in their analysis on a given threat issue, before such errors can have fateful consequences. The panels should thus oversee all the testing. And, to be effective on a given issue, a panel should include experts not only in the subject matter but also in collection and methodology.

Absent compelling evidence, the dominant view on an issue is generally based on the assumption or judgment that it is most likely correct—not proof that it is. Such conventional wisdom will sometimes be correct, but sometimes not. Given this uncertainty and mindful that on some issues error could be costly, the proposed process for alternative analysis simply says to analysts: here is a way to rigorously examine conventional wisdom on a case-by-case basis and determine whether it or some other view is probably correct. And when done as the need arises, intelligence will be better able to provide key national security customers with clear, timely, and well-substantiated warning.

Notes

1 Originally published by Karl Spielmann, "Strengthening Intelligence Threat Analysis," *International Journal of Intelligence and Counterintelligence*, vol. 25, no. 1, Spring 2012, pp. 19–43. Reprinted by permission of Taylor & Francis Ltd, www.tandfonline.com.

2 The highly publicized controversies over the past decade and more have covered a span of issues, including enhanced collection techniques particularly involving the practice and legality of water boarding; the role and limitations of the Foreign Intelligence Surveillance Act (FISA) court for certain National Security Agency (NSA) collection; and, in the law enforcement realm, the issue of whether terrorist suspects should be accorded Miranda rights.

3 Ironically, the successful operation against Osama bin Laden on May 1, 2011 may heighten expectations in the intelligence and national security communities—as well as among the general public—of what intelligence analysis should be able to achieve on a regular basis. Publicly available information indicates that collection clearly played a key role in the operation that eliminated Al Qaida's leader but that skillful and persistent analysis also contributed. In comments that echo the National Commission on Terrorist Attacks Upon the United States (9/11 Commission)'s emphasis on the importance and difficulty of "connecting the dots," John Brennan, President Obama's top advisor at the time on counter terrorism, according to an Associated Press story "… told CNN … 'there was no single piece of information that was an "ah-hah" moment. He said officials took "bits and pieces" of intelligence gathered and analyzed over a long time to nail down the leads they needed.'" See Associated Press, "Phone Call by Kuwaiti Courier Led to Bin Laden," May 3, 2011: http://abcnews.go.com/US/wireStory?id=13512344.

4 See Preface, note 3.

5 See Preface, note 4.

6 Upheavals in Tunisia, Egypt, Libya, and other countries in the Middle East and North Africa beginning in December 2010 raised fresh questions about whether and to what extent intelligence was able to predict these events. Publicly available information is not adequate to permit anything more than speculative judgments to be made on an unclassified level. The techniques discussed in this article, however, do suggest a number of questions to help appropriately cleared individuals assess the intelligence analysis leading up to these events— beginning with whether alternative views were raised *and* seriously tested. See also Chapter 1, p. 3.

7 The key document underpinning the role of the analytic quality component in the Office of the Director of National Intelligence (DNI) is *Intelligence Community Directive Number 203: Analytic Standards*, January 2, 2015: www.fas.org/irp/dni/icd/icd-203.pdf.

8 As an example of the IC's use of such venues, see the CIA's website for a chronology of key CIA Directorate of Intelligence (DI) milestones, including setting up a "Red Cell" in the DI in the wake of the 9/11 attacks. The WMD Commission report, which dealt with the later failure to find WMD as expected in Iraq, strongly endorsed the use of such "red cell" efforts as a means to have alternative views considered or "generated." But it did not emphasize that it is hardly sufficient to just come up with hypotheses. Rather—in accord with good standard practice in both the physical and social sciences—it is *also* necessary to then proceed to test them. See, Government Publishing Office, *Unclassified Version of the Report of the Commission on the Intelligence Capabilities of the United States Regarding Weapons of Mass Destruction*, March 31, 2005: www.gpo.gov/fdsys/pkg/GPO-WMD/pdf/GPO-WMD.pdf, p. 569. See also Chapter 1, note 2.

9 A useful and fair description of the Team A/Team B competitive analysis exercise can be found on the Internet site Wikipedia under the title Team B. See also Chapter 1, note 18.

10 As one example of an approach that picked up on the "connecting the dots" theme post 9/11 (see also note 3) and that emphasized the importance and great difficulty of coping effectively with large and diffuse bodies of data, see the RAND website for Hollywood et al.'s "'Connecting the Dots' in Intelligence: Detecting Terrorist Threats in the Out-of-the Ordinary," RAND Brief, RAND Corporation, Santa Monica, CA, 2005: www.rand.org/pubs/research_briefs/ RB9079.html.

11 The eighteenth century philosophers David Hume and Immanuel Kant, for example, had very different views of the relationship between concepts and evidence. Hume discounted earlier notions of "laws of nature" and argued that what we took to be laws were really habitual associations that certain empirical data prompted us to make. Kant did not concede empirical data to have such a determining role in our thinking. He contended that the human mind was capable of devising concepts on its own to impose order on what would otherwise be just a kaleidoscope of sensory impressions. (Hume's classic work, which spells out his key epistemological assumptions, is "A Treatise of Human Nature," in Frederick Watkins ed., *Hume: Theory of Politics*, Nelson Press, Edinburgh, 1951. Kant's main concepts are presented in the "Critique of Pure Speculative Reason" and the "Critique of Pure Practical Reason," excerpts of which are in Carl J. Friedrich ed., *Immanuel Kant's Moral and Political Writings*, The Modern Library, New York, 1949.) See also Chapter 1, note 3.

12 The National Commission on Terrorist Attacks Upon the United States (9/11 Commission), in commenting on the failure of the U.S. government to "connect the dots" and have any real appreciation of the attacks being planned, flatly stated that "the most important failure was one of imagination." See discussion of general findings in the *Report of the National Commission on Terrorist Attacks Upon the United States* available on website for the National Commission on Terrorist Attacks Upon the United States archived in 2004. For the full final report see www.9-11commission.gov/report/911Report.pdf. Chapter 11 ("Foresight—and Hindsight") provides additional discussion of institutionalizing imagination, especially the case of aircraft as weapons (pp. 344–348).

13 Chapter 8 of the final *Report of the National Commission on Terrorist Attacks Upon the United States* ("The System Was Blinking Red") has various discussions of "suspicious flight training" issues, including an FBI memo from their Phoenix field office in July 2001; flight training by one of the plotters (Moussaoui) beginning in February 2001; and even a comment by one of the FBI's field supervisors that, in calling attention to Moussaoui's training, he was "trying to keep someone from taking a plane and crashing it into the World Trade Center." See www.9-11commission.gov/report/9-11Report.pdf, pp. 272–276.

14 See Chapter 1, note 2 and Robert Jervis, "Reports, Politics, and Intelligence Failures: The Case of Iraq," *The Journal of Strategic Studies*, vol. 29, no. 1, February 2006, p. 17.

15 See especially Anthony Cave Brown, *Bodyguard of Lies*, Harper & Row, New York, 1975.

16 As discussed in the text, an invalid hypothesis should be lacking important supporting data. And it is sensible for analysts to assume this when data are

missing, unless denial efforts can be identified. The Sherlock Holmes short story, *Silver Blaze* (in *The Memoirs of Sherlock Holmes*, Dover Thrift Editions, Mineola, NY, 2010), featuring "the dog that didn't bark" is a famous example of missing data pointing to an invalid hypothesis. In the story the key issue was whether the culprit in the case was a stranger or someone with whom the dog on the scene was familiar. Its barking would have indicated the culprit was a stranger and there is no indication in the story that the dog was muzzled or tranquilized to deny such information to any investigators. Barking simply was absent when it would have been expected to occur. Therefore, a hypothesis that the culprit was a stranger was invalidated because it lacked important supporting data.

17 The expression "absence of evidence is not (necessarily) evidence of absence" has been popularized by such diverse figures as the scientist Carl Sagan and former Secretary of Defense Donald Rumsfeld. It is also appropriate to note that, for sorting out the denial issue, the expression is an important caution about jumping to a wrong conclusion but hardly the last word. It is no more valid for analysts who may be prone to suspect denial to jump to the conclusion that "absence of evidence is (necessarily) evidence of presence." The possibility of denial simply needs further investigation as the proposed enhanced analytic technique seeks to do.

18 The classic treatment of the topic is by the German sociologist, Max Weber (see, for example, H.H. Gerth [with C. Wright Mills], *From Max Weber: Essays in Sociology*, Oxford University Press, New York, 1946). Weber saw the inherent conservatism of bureaucracies as having not only certain drawbacks but also as having the plus side of being essentially a force for stability. He contrasted situations wherein bureaucracies played a large role in governing with situations in which more personalized rule held sway.

19 Heuer and many other methodologists have long paid close attention to cognitive biases as a key factor affecting whether analysts are likely "to get it right." See also Chapter 1, notes 7 and 8.

20 One of the key documents addressing analytic issues is the WMD Commission report (see note 8). This report underscored the issue of misplaced confidence in consistency in noting that: "When we reviewed finished intelligence, we found egregious examples of poor tradecraft, such as using a piece of evidence to support an argument when the same piece also supported exactly the opposite argument—and failing to note this fact." (p. 408). See also Chapter 1, pp. 13–14.

21 Robert Jervis's analysis on the Iraqi WMD issue has important implications for judging what views should qualify in a shared consistency test as potential competitors of a dominant view—and therefore merit further testing in a subsequent inconsistency test. Does one, for example, discount a view that entails seemingly irrational behavior by the adversary, such as Saddam displayed by discontinuing his WMD efforts but not dispelling U.S. concerns about them? Jervis argues, both in a recent book (see note 23) and in an earlier review of the WMD failure and the post mortems on it (see note 14), that no alternative explanations would likely have seemed as plausible as the prevailing intelligence view on Iraqi WMD.

22 Jack Davis, *Improving CIA Analytic Performance: Strategic Warning*, Occasional Papers, vol. 1, no. 1, Sherman Kent Center for Intelligence Analysis, U.S. Central Intelligence Agency, September 2002.

23 Robert Jervis, *Why Intelligence Fails: Lessons from the Iranian Revolution and the Iraq War*, Cornell University Press, Ithaca, NY, 2010.
24 See Chapter 8 of the final *Report of the National Commission on Terrorist Attacks Upon the United States* (see note 12).
25 The rankings based on toting up inconsistencies and key missing data can also be very transparent, so the basis for the probability judgments is well understood by all potential audiences. For each hypothesis that is tested, the rankings would show the mix of assessed inconsistencies and missing data and the test charts would show the specific inconsistencies and missing data involved. See also Chapter 1, note 12.
26 Recurring cycles of intelligence failures and lessons learned from them underscore that key analytic problem areas—such as cognitive biases or foreign D&D—are not diseases that some vaccine might eventually eradicate. As the techniques proposed here are intended to do, one can only realistically hope to chip away at these sorts of problems and reduce (not eliminate) the chances for error on major issues such as threats.

Bibliography

Associated Press, "Phone Call by Kuwaiti Courier Led to Bin Laden," May 3, 2011: http://abcnews.go.com/US/wirestory?id=13512344.

Brown, Anthony Cave, *Bodyguard of Lies*, Harper & Row, New York, 1975.

Davis, Jack, *Improving CIA Analytic Performance: Strategic Warning*, Occasional Papers, vol. 1, no. 1, Sherman Kent Center for Intelligence Analysis, U.S. Central Intelligence Agency, September 2002.

Doyle, Sir Arthur Conan, *The Memoirs of Sherlock Holmes*, Dover Thrift Editions, Mineola, NY, 2010.

Gerth, H.H. (with C. Wright Mills), *From Max Weber: Essays in Sociology*, Oxford University Press, New York, 1946.

Government Publishing Office, *Unclassified Version of the Report of the Commission on the Intelligence Capabilities of the United States Regarding Weapons of Mass Destruction*, March 31, 2005: www.gpo.gov/fdsys/pkg/GPO-WMD/pdf/GPO-WMD.pdf.

Heuer, Richards J., *Psychology of Intelligence Analysis*, Kindle ed., Center for the Study of Intelligence, Central Intelligence Agency, Washington, DC, 2016.

Heuer, Richards J. (with Randolph H. Pherson), *Structured Analytic Techniques for Intelligence Analysis*, 2nd ed., CQ Press, Los Angeles, 2014.

Hollywood, John S. (with Diane Snyder, Kenneth N. McKay, and John E. Boon, Jr.), " 'Connecting the Dots' in Intelligence: Detecting Terrorist Threats in the Out-of-the-Ordinary," RAND Brief, RAND Corporation, Santa Monica, CA, 2005: www.rand.org/pubs/research_briefs/RB9079.html.

Hume, David, "A Treatise of Human Nature," in Frederick Watkins ed., *Hume: Theory of Politics*, Nelson Press, Edinburgh, 1951.

Jervis, Robert, "Reports, Politics, and Intelligence Failures: The Case of Iraq," *The Journal of Strategic Studies*, vol. 29, no. 1, February 2006, pp. 3–52.

Jervis, Robert, *Why Intelligence Fails: Lessons from the Iranian Revolution and the Iraq War*, Cornell University Press, Ithaca, NY, 2010.

Kant, Immanuel, "Critique of Pure Speculative Reason" and "Critique of Pure Practical Reason," in Carl J. Friedrich ed., *Immanuel Kant's Moral and Political Writings*, The Modern Library, New York, 1949.

National Commission on Terrorist Attacks Upon the United States, *Report of the National Commission on Terrorist Attacks Upon the United States*, Final Report, July 22, 2004: www.9-11commission.gov/report/911Report.pdf.

Office of the Director of National Intelligence, *Intelligence Community Directive Number 203: Analytic Standards*, January 2, 2015: www.fas.org/irp/dni/icd/icd-203.pdf.

Popper, Sir Karl, *Conjectures and Refutations: The Growth of Scientific Knowledge*, Routledge Classics, London, 2000.

Spielmann, Karl, "Strengthening Intelligence Threat Analysis," *International Journal of Intelligence and Counterintelligence*, vol. 25, no. 1, Spring 2012, pp. 19–43.

3 Using enhanced analytic techniques for threat analysis

A case study illustration[1]

This is intended as an instructional supplement to the methodology presented in Chapter 2 (originally published in the article "Strengthening Intelligence Threat Analysis"[2]) Through the presentation of a hypothetical case study, it aims to facilitate analysts' use of that proposed methodology by walking them through the major tests that comprise its assessment process.

Accurately determining the nature and likelihood of a terrorist or state actor threat can be very difficult, with high costs for failure. This proposed methodology is a tool to help analysts better provide clear, timely, and well-substantiated warning to key decision makers. Its assessment process has three successive tests, which build on each other to determine strengths and weaknesses of different possible views on a threat. The first two tests yield important interim results, affording early intelligence inputs for decision making. When completed, the testing provides a numerical basis for ranking competing views, enabling more precise and transparent judgments to be made on a threat's probability than is common practice.

In general, the testing process incorporating the enhanced analytic techniques requires in turn: first, the zero-based review to assess the strengths and weaknesses of a dominant view on a threat (featuring a test of whether it <u>shares</u> consistency); second, the new amplified inconsistency test to ensure key available data are not overlooked[3] and to double-check source vetting to detect deception; and finally, the missing data test to identify critical missing data for the hypotheses and to detect foreign denial. The culmination is a ranking of the hypotheses based on assessed inconsistencies and missing data needs that constitute overall validation tasks for each competing view. The hypothesis with the fewest overall tasks has the strongest claim to validity.

A hypothetical case study to show how enhanced analytic techniques can be used

Why hypothetical?

In an open discussion, how the proposed assessment process might be used in dissecting a real intelligence issue cannot be shown—particularly to do so in detail, which makes the use of even historical cases inadvisable.[4] To enable the methodology's key benefits and demands to be better understood however, a scenario is provided that is hypothetical but realistic and shows how alternative explanations and various relevant data could be tested. The scenario posits a dominant intelligence view on a military problem with important national security ramifications—a view that turns out to be seriously flawed when challenged.

The scenario

Country X possesses certain special military capabilities. Surrounded by perceived adversaries, X is concerned these capabilities could be attacked and destroyed. X is therefore presumed to have tried to mitigate their vulnerability. While there has been a mainstream intelligence view for some time on X's chosen course of action to deal with the vulnerability problem, other views now dispute it. All parties recognize X's choice could have important national security implications for the U.S. and other countries. To provide needed guidance as to which course of action is most and least likely, investigators are using a zero-based review, then an inconsistency test with a rebuttal process, and finally a missing data test so that the alternatives can be ranked. The investigators appreciate that important interim findings will be available as each test is completed. Thus, even before concluding overall testing, they can provide timely intelligence inputs on the issue for concerned decision makers.

Some guideposts and tips for analysts

1   As stated, the method comprises three separate interconnected tests. The **inconsistency test** builds on the **zero-based review**; the **missing data test** builds on the inconsistency test. This means analysts should not try to take the latter tests out of context.
2   The testing involves a lot of hypotheses and data sets so that hypothesis testing can be as effective as possible. Overall, there are eight hypotheses, eight sets of available data to test them for inconsistencies, and five sets to test the same hypotheses for critical missing data.

In a computerized version, which I cannot provide here, these hypotheses and data sets doubtless would be quite easy to handle. As it is, in this written presentation, analysts regrettably have many acronyms to juggle. There are, however, only four acronyms that figure heavily in the story: the Dominant Conventional view hypothesis **(DC)**; its main supporting data, Long Known Information **(LKI)**; the New Recent Challenge view hypothesis **(NRC)**: and its main supporting data, Direct Knowledgeable Information **(DKI)**.

3   The discussion starts with laying out all the hypotheses and data sets that are used in the inconsistency test, so analysts can know up front what will eventually be covered there. Obviously, in real life this would not be the case—various hypotheses and supporting data would emerge as analysts appreciate the need to come up with alternatives to a dominant view and argue for them.

4   Treatment of "shared consistency" as a source of error is a big feature in my overall methodology since it seems less obvious than the problem of inconsistency (which Popper, Heuer, and other methodologists have extensively treated). Dealing with shared consistency of data with more than one hypothesis (which is the full term) is partly done in the first stage of testing, the **zero-based review**. Analysts can discover there that it can undercut a dominant view's claim to validity. But the seriousness of shared consistency is only truly revealed when analysts, in coming up with alternative views in the second stage of testing, the **inconsistency test**, can assess how widely the sharing occurs.

5   Analysts can expect to find more background material in the third stage of testing, the **missing data test** discussion because, compared to inconsistency testing, this is likely to be their initial exposure to such a test. For example, I lay out there the rationale for why a missing data test is needed to complement an inconsistency test, how one goes about determining what data are missing for various hypotheses, and where the denial issue fits into the picture.

Posited hypotheses and data

Since the methodology aims to test more hypotheses and bodies of data than standard intelligence tests, it necessarily will burden readers with more acronyms in discussing the testing process.

Hypotheses. Reflecting the importance of using many hypotheses, the investigators generate eight for testing. At one extreme, a dominant conventional (DC) view of many years standing argues that X relied on certain evident protective measures to mitigate the vulnerability of the special capabilities. At the other extreme, a major new recent challenge (NRC) view argues that X took certain unexpected measures that are not evident to mitigate the vulnerability while seeking to have adversaries focus on the evident measures. The other views are: do nothing (DN); rely, respectively, on other key capabilities (OKC), other lesser capabilities (OLC), reinforcement (R), natural phenomena (NP), and movement (M).

Data sets. The investigators also use eight sets of the relevant available data to test the hypotheses. At one extreme, long known information (LKI) comprises a large body of circumstantial and observational data from which widely accepted inferences have been drawn over the years about X's course of action, reflected in the dominant conventional (DC) view. At the other extreme, direct knowledgeable insider information (DKII) is direct evidence, recently acquired by technical means, which supports the new recent challenge (NRC) view. (Because of the potential importance of this evidence, the collector performed a risk assessment that concluded compromise of this collection—and thus its manipulation by country X for deception—was unlikely. These favorable vetting results for DKII were not included as a separate data set in the inconsistency test, but were considered with the test to be double-checked.) Other data sets are: separate later production data (SLPD); data on X's knowledge (XK); data on lax protective measures (LPM); separate later production data exceeding (SLPDE); separate older production data exceeding (SOPDE); and feasibility assessment data (FA).

The zero-based review in the hypothetical scenario

To set the stage for the inconsistency and missing data tests, the investigators first subject the dominant view to a zero-based review to evaluate whether it is fundamentally sound or has major weaknesses. Backers of a dominant view—both analysts and their superiors who have signed onto it—may otherwise be reluctant to consider subjecting it to an inconsistency test with alternative views. If major weaknesses are found, prudence would dictate that they reconsider. To start, the investigators conduct a basic scrub of the dominant view's underpinnings, that is, the overall body of evidence as well as the reasoning supporting this view. And they expect analysts who endorse it to help provide this information.

A zero-based review basic scrub

A zero-based review seeks to judge a dominant view solely on its merits to see whether its standing claim to be the correct view holds up. Except when there is general agreement that this claim rests on truly compelling evidence, various questions—basically, 10 in all—are relevant for such a review. On evidence: How much evidence supports the dominant view?

How varied is the evidence? Is most of it recent or could it now be dated? Is some or much of the evidence direct, such as from some insider source or sources? If so, how thoroughly has it been checked to see if it could be phony—either directed from the target or a personal fabrication? Is the evidence mainly or solely circumstantial and thus potentially more susceptible to different interpretations? If so, has any effort been made to check out other potential interpretations of such circumstantial evidence? (This can be a pivotal question, as the examination of the "shared consistency" problem indicates below.) On reasoning: Is the logic of the overall case sound? Have key assumptions been addressed—and reexamined over time? And a final question focuses on a unique concern of this methodology: Has the impact of missing data been assessed?

The relevance of several of these questions shows that a zero-based review can help reveal whether a dominant view is weakly or strongly supported—irrespective of how long or how widely it has been accepted as the conventional wisdom on an intelligence issue. The critical question to be probed, however, is whether its main supporting data are solely consistent with the dominant view or whether this consistency is (or could be) shared with other views. This question can be pivotal in determining whether a dominant view has a deserved edge over competitors.

Consistency is better than inconsistency, but watch out

As shown in detail below, because the DC view is consistent with the most voluminous body of data, long known information (LKI), this consistency seems at the outset to provide powerful support for the DC view. But if other views could also be consistent with LKI, the DC view is weaker than originally assumed, because each of these other views would have an equal claim to validity based on this evidence. (Ultimately, it turns out that, when the inconsistency test is later held, seven other views qualify—reducing DC to a "1-in-8" shot to be correct based on it.) A central objective of a zero-based review, therefore, is to see whether a dominant view can support its standing claim to be the correct view by showing it is exclusively consistent with its main supporting evidence—in this case LKI. If it cannot—and if additional weaknesses are revealed in the basic scrub discussed above—there would be a strong *prima facie* case for the dominant view to undergo an inconsistency test.

A first cut at the shared consistency problem

For a zero-based review, a dominant view does not have to try to demonstrate its consistency is exclusive by specifically identifying all of the contenders it might eventually face in an inconsistency test. It does have to show, however, that it is has carefully considered the circumstances in which one or more potential competitors might share consistency. And it might be able to show there are no plausible circumstances in which this could happen. In this scenario, however, common ground is available for other views to claim consistency with LKI. LKI comprises multiple indicators of evident protective measures for the special capabilities, which DC regards as making the case that X is relying on these measures. But what if X were relying on other means to protect the special capabilities and viewed the evident protective measures as merely a backup to them or even a diversion? Wouldn't the analyst expect to see the same indicators that the evident protective measures exist? On their face, such circumstances could not reasonably be ruled out.

To fully demonstrate DC's weakness, this case now discusses more comprehensively—perhaps more than a zero-based review would normally require—the evidence LKI embodies and its susceptibility to multiple interpretations. Certain other issues that a basic scrub would raise—such as the importance of questioning other assumptions—are treated as well.

A dominant view's data support: what a zero-based review can show

Because of the importance of the shared consistency issue, an elaboration on how the dominant conventional (DC) view could lose its proprietary hold on the long known information (LKI) data set is in order. To show that certain real world dominant views might plausibly share this vulnerability, it is useful to flesh out some of the characteristics that can be reasonably posited for LKI as support for DC.

Apparent strengths in LKI's support for DC. LKI has been made by far the most voluminous data set among the various data sets considered in the scenario. The DC view also has been favored by resting it on a very logical assumption about what the data indicate—namely, since the evident protective measures are associated with the special capabilities, that X must be relying on these measures to protect the special capabilities would seem obvious.

Weaknesses in LKI's support for DC. LKI has been made a large body of circumstantial evidence, as many large bodies of supporting evidence would tend to be in the real world. Circumstantial evidence, by its nature, is likely to be open to more interpretations on some issue than direct evidence. LKI has also been made a body of evidence that is primarily observational data, as would a very large body of data for intelligence analysis. This data provides multiple indications of the special capabilities and evident protective measures. As such, analysts certainly can use the data to try to deduce what in X's basic decisions may have resulted in these capabilities and measures. But the observational data are not direct evidence of the decisions themselves.

A preview: NRC in perspective. To highlight the importance of DC's dependence on this body of circumstantial and observational data, it is useful to note that when the inconsistency test is later held, DC as well as its competitors lack the support of direct evidence except for the new recent challenge (NRC) view. That hypothesis is backed by direct evidence, which explicitly contradicts DC. DC's fundamental weakness, however, is not that it is opposed by direct evidence, although that is obviously significant. Rather, the shortcoming is that other hypotheses can be consistent with the circumstantial and observational evidence DC relies on for its support. Even if NRC were left totally out of the picture in the inconsistency test, DC would still face six other competitors consistent with LKI—reducing it to a 1-in-7 shot to be correct based on LKI instead of a 1-in-8 shot with NRC included.

The key test in the zero-based review. As my earlier *IJIC* article (Chapter 2) discussed, a dominant view cannot be expected to detail all its potential competitors prior to an inconsistency test. Yet, a dominant view does have to seriously demonstrate that it has tried to determine whether its claimed consistency with its main supporting data is exclusive. And a reasonable way to do that is by a <u>shared consistency test</u> to probe whether there could be plausible circumstances in which other views could be consistent. Can DC, therefore, show that it has made such an inquiry with regard to LKI and found that no plausible circumstances exist? Unfortunately for DC, such circumstances exist. Any hypotheses challenging DC—and claiming that X was relying on other means to protect the special capabilities—would have to explain why, if X was not relying on them, the evident protective measures would even exist. Such hypotheses could contend logically that the measures are a backup for the measures they propose, or (as NRC's direct evidence later shows in the inconsistency test) serve as a diversion. Backup or diversionary roles for the evident protective measures would clearly be a different take than DC has on LKI. But they could still account for why, over the years, there have been multiple indicators of the evident protective measures associated with the special capabilities which constitute LKI.

A battle of inferences. The kind of evidence that LKI embodies makes any contest with other views that could claim consistency with LKI basically a battle of inferences. Except for NRC's ability to draw on direct evidence in the later inconsistency test, the nature of LKI would pit inferences drawn by DC about what the data say against inferences drawn by other hypotheses about what the data say. Other hypotheses (including NRC) would not be disputing that the observational data provide numerous indications of the special capabilities and the evident protective measures. They would simply be differing with DC over what are the supportable inferences to be drawn from these data. Whereas DC infers that the evident protective measures are the logical choice for X, other hypotheses—claiming to offer other, better means of protection—would be inferring the evident protective measures would not have been a good choice for X.

Another questionable assumption. In showing that DC has a misplaced confidence about its singular consistency with LKI, the review highlights a major faulty assumption of DC's case. But the review also identifies another critical assumption that could be faulty. This involves the fact that for X to depend on measures it knew to be ineffective would be self-defeating. Thus, DC would have to assume that X believed adversaries were unaware of the evident protective measures or that adversaries were aware but unable to counter them. But does evidence support this? Certainly in an inconsistency test, other competitors would challenge DC.

Bottom line. Overall, other hypotheses could claim to be at least as consistent as DC with LKI, with both sides simply drawing different inferences from the same body of data. This finding, and other zero-based review results, could serve as the first major intelligence input for decision makers deliberating X's course on the special capabilities' vulnerability. Since all views would be equally valid based on LKI alone, this impasse needs to be resolved by bringing in additional relevant data for an inconsistency test. As the chart for that test shows, additional data are posited that directly bear on the issues concerning LKI that the zero-based review reveals. In particular, data on X's knowledge (XK) shows X knew adversaries were aware of and could counter the evident protective measures; data on lax protective measures (LPM) shows implementation of these measures was lax, belying DC's claim of X depending on them. Thus, DC is inconsistent with both data sets—all other views are consistent.

The new inconsistency test in the hypothetical scenario

Some key features

With the results of the zero-based review in hand, indicating the dominant view has no special edge when competing with alternative views, the investigators proceed to lay out eight hypotheses and eight data sets for an inconsistency test (see Table 3.1). This test, as emphasized in my earlier published *IJIC* article (Chapter 2), is similar to the test in Heuer's Analysis of Competing Hypotheses (ACH) methodology, but has more hypotheses and incorporates vetting results (albeit, in this illustration, as a supplement). Because the test also provides for a robust rebuttal effort when the assessments of inconsistencies have been made, it is generally more streamlined than in the ACH version, which seeks to further filter the initial inconsistency determinations. Such filtering, however, can best be accomplished in the give and take of a rebuttal effort and, for high impact intelligence issues, with a panel of outside reviewers overseeing it to ensure balance and rigor—as recommended in Chapter 2.

To keep the chart simple, only the investigators' bottom line assessments of inconsistencies are provided. In any real world inconsistency test, of course, key reasons for each assessment in the chart would be presented in an accompanying text. (An accompanying text with such rationales is demonstrated below in the less familiar missing data test.)

Nevertheless, the reasons for the investigators' (consistency) assessments on LKI already have been provided in the zero-based review. Also useful is an elaboration of the inconsistency assessments for DC based on the data sets X's knowledge (XK) and lax protective measures (LPM). These data sets are singled out because they show data that may be readily at hand could plausibly go unnoticed with a single view holding sway. As such, they help to illustrate why using many hypotheses is important to help ensure available data are not ignored.

- For XK, information showing that X knew adversaries were aware of, and could counter, the evident protective measures might be readily available from open or classified documents at hand. But if analysts had no strong incentive to question X's knowledge—until DC was challenged by other views—they might well pay little attention to such documents.
- For LPM, information on laxity in implementing the protective measures might only require taking a careful chronological look at the historical record of LKI data. But, again, if analysts had no strong incentive to question their assumptions about X relying on these measures—until DC was challenged by other views—they might well have little reason to carry out such a review.

How the chart is laid out

The chart shows how the contending views narrow down based on the inconsistency assessments. Because diverse bodies of data cannot be reliably weighted, all inconsistencies are treated as equally important.[5] Certain data

Table 3.1 Investigators' table: which hypotheses are inconsistent with key data?

Hypotheses	DC	DN	OKC	OLC	R	NP	M	NRC
Data sets								
LKI	no	no	no	no	no	no	no	no
SLPD	no	no	no	no	no	no	no	no
XK	yes	no	no	no	no	no	no	no
LPM	yes	no	no	no	no	no	no	no
SLPDE	yes	yes	yes	yes	yes	yes	no	no
SOPDE	yes	yes	yes	yes	yes	yes	yes	no
FA	yes	yes	yes	yes	yes	yes	yes	no
DKII	yes	yes	yes	yes	yes	yes	yes	no

Posited hypotheses

DC (dominant conventional): X relied over the years on certain evident protective measures to mitigate the vulnerability of certain special capabilities.

DN (do nothing): X decided to do nothing substantial in peacetime to mitigate their vulnerability (expecting any measures to be countered) but, faced with an imminent threat, to use the special capabilities before they could be destroyed.

OKC (other key capabilities): X looked to other key and more secure capabilities, hitherto unknown to adversaries, to compensate for the special capabilities' vulnerability.

OLC (other lesser capabilities): X looked to other lesser but more secure capabilities, already known to adversaries, to compensate for the special capabilities' vulnerability.

R (reinforcement): X reinforced the special capability installations, using standard reinforcement measures.

NP (natural phenomena): X looked to certain well-known natural phenomena on its territory to mitigate the special capabilities' vulnerability.

M (movement): X surreptitiously provided for some additional special capabilities in more recent years in order to be able to move them and thus protect them if a threat loomed.

NRC (new recent challenge): X relied on certain unexpected measures over the years to prevent detection of some special capabilities, while seeking to have adversaries focus on evident protective measures.

Posited data sets

LKI (long known information): numerous indications of X's special capabilities and evident measures to protect them.

SLPD (separate later production data): production data in later years in apparent conformity with the DC take on the size and nature of the special capabilities (but, as with LKI, actually consistent with multiple hypotheses).

XK (X's knowledge): data on X's knowledge that evident protective measures in LKI could be countered.

LPM (lax protective measures): data on laxity in implementing the evident protective measures in LKI.

SLPDE (separate later production data exceeding): production data in later years exceeding the DC take on the special capabilities.

SOPDE (separate older production data exceeding): earlier production data exceeding the DC take.

FA (feasibility assessment): assessment indicating the basic feasibility of the unexpected measures to protect vulnerable capabilities specified in DKII.

DKII (direct knowledgeable insider information): recent data underpinning the NRC view.

merit special attention simply as drivers of the winnowing process—they help distinguish between hypotheses and are thus diagnostic. XK and LPM qualify: they separate DC from all other views. Other drivers include:

- The data set designated separate later production data exceeding (SLPDE), which indicates X made recent provisions for special capabilities in excess of the detected capabilities' needs. This further narrows the competition to the movement (M) and new recent challenge (NRC) views. They posit undetected special capabilities consistent with such provisions; the other views do not.
- The data set separate older production data exceeding (SOPDE), which in turn separates the new recent challenge (NRC) hypothesis from the movement (M) hypothesis. M is not consistent with X making early (as well as recent) provisions for undetected capabilities, but NRC is. (And, NRC ultimately is also the only view lacking inconsistencies with the two remaining data sets.)

Inconsistency test results and next steps

Results. Overall, the new inconsistency test illustrated in the scenario shows that:

- With no inconsistencies, the new recent challenge (NRC) view is the strongest hypothesis thus far. Also, its lack of any inconsistencies with eight bodies of diverse data is a reliable double-check that the direct evidence (DKII) supporting it probably is not deceptive. (As Chapter 2 discusses, a target would find it difficult to manipulate multiple, diverse data to lend credence to a source's lie.)
- Most of the remaining hypotheses are significantly weaker, and also may have other individual shortcomings, registering inconsistencies with about half of the common bodies of data.
- The posited longstanding dominant conventional (DC) approach qualifies as the weakest contender thus far, registering inconsistencies with six of the eight common bodies of data. This means that to claim validity in the future it would face the most severe challenge. It would have to explain away a wide range of assessed inconsistencies to deal not only with the much better performance of the new recent challenge view (NRC) on the test but also the better performances of the six other contenders.

To help ensure that concerned decision makers get timely intelligence inputs as the testing process proceeds, the investigators could provide these inconsistency test results to them as important interim findings. These results could be presented as a major step in reaching judgments on the validity of the different views on X's course of action. If time were truly of the essence for decision making, the zero-based review results, of course, would have afforded even earlier help.

Implications for U.S. national security could also be pointed out. Probably the most important implication at this point would be that (contrary to what DC has long purported) little to no confidence should be maintained for U.S. planning that intelligence knows the vulnerability or even the size of X's special capabilities. The strength of NRC is one reason such high uncertainty is warranted. Another results from the extreme weakness of DC and (NRC aside) the emergence of six other serious contenders.

Follow up. Next steps in the inquiry (including which concerned decision makers could also be informed) would entail efforts to secure key missing data and dealing with rebuttals to the inconsistency assessments. How and when rebuttals would be made could vary. By its nature, a dominant view is likely to have a considerable number of personal and institutional stakeholders in the "correctness" of this position, thus almost guaranteeing that any inconsistency call will be highly contentious. Thus, given expected challenges to the inconsistency test findings, engaging a panel of outside reviewers to evaluate the inconsistency calls and the rejoinders to them to ensure balanced and rigorous treatment would be useful. (And, as earlier emphasized, since the zero-based review and missing data test findings may also be challenged, such a panel might oversee these tests as well for high impact threat issues, such as this case involves.)

The hypothetical case also illustrates the scope of the challenge that rebuttals could face. Even if assuming that DC alone sought to make rebuttals—and no other views tried—it would have to win two of six potential contests to pull even with five of the other hypotheses; it would have to win three to tie the hypothesis in second place; and it would need to win all six contests to tie with NRC.

Contesting other views' consistency assessments, of course, would be another way for DC to improve its relative standing. But at best DC would only gain the status of being one of many very weak hypotheses. It would still have to rebut its own inconsistencies to claim validity.

The rankings based on the inconsistency test are preliminary in any case, because all hypotheses must undergo a missing data test that can add requirements for each to claim validity. And, as is shown, the missing data test results do change the relative standing of some hypotheses (notably, the Other Key Capabilities [OKC] and Movement [M] hypotheses lose status).

The missing data test in the hypothetical scenario

Identifying critical types of missing data and priorities for data searches

Setting up a missing data test involves taking the competing hypotheses on a given intelligence issue and arraying them against a check list of generic types of data that are relevant for that issue—as suggested by the claims and extant support each hypothesis has brought to the table in the inconsistency test. (The relevant data types will, of course, differ somewhat for a military issue, political issue, economic issue, and so on.) In particular, the inconsistency test alerts investigators to key considerations for identifying the most significant types of missing data for individual hypotheses. For example, as this case later amplifies:

- Since one hypothesis (NRC, the strongest one thus far) has direct evidence from an insider source to support it and the other views do not, this would obviously be difficult for other views to counter unless they too could secure such direct evidence in their behalf.
- Also, since a number of hypotheses posit the existence of various capabilities, they would all have an evident need to establish this—such as by observational data or at least by feasibility assessments indicating that these capabilities reasonably could exist.

The inconsistency test also alerts the investigators to considerations that help them determine the appropriate priority for seeking missing data. They believe they can identify data that are critical and should be sought currently and data that may be needed in the future. For example:

- The hypothesis supported by direct evidence (NRC) has had that evidence both favorably vetted and favorably double-checked by the inconsistency test—and, as noted above, faces competitors lacking any direct evidence to support their view. Under these circumstances, the first priority would be for the competitors to come up with such evidence. Securing further corroboration for NRC's direct evidence would be less critical but could be a future missing data task.

Setting an overall validation standard

The investigators' ultimate aim in the missing data test is to build on the inconsistency test and establish an overall standard for analysis when truly compelling evidence is lacking to provide proof that a given view is correct. In these fairly common circumstances for analysis, full validation would basically impose two sets of tasks on a hypothesis: (1) to rebut assessed inconsistencies; and (2) to secure critical data judged to be missing. The number of overall tasks for each hypothesis then provides the basis for ranking them (see Table 3.3).

In ranking hypotheses, should a body of missing data have the same importance as an inconsistency as a liability for a hypothesis? Probably not. But, as with different inconsistencies, there is no reliable way to weight them with any precision.[6] Nonetheless, because an inconsistency is based on data in hand that can be scrutinized, giving an inconsistency generally greater weight in a head-to-head match up with a missing data item would be prudent. Thus, if two hypotheses have the same number of validation tasks but the second one has more inconsistencies, the latter should be seen as somewhat weaker. (As shown in Table 3.3, the overall validation tasks in this case provide such examples: two hypotheses emerge tied for "basically" a distant second place, but one of them actually has fewer inconsistencies than the others.) However, the distinction between an inconsistency and missing data item is likely to really matter only if the two hypotheses are vying to be the strongest hypothesis in the rankings, probably a rare occurrence.

Even for the strongest hypothesis some of the validation tasks might never be accomplished; for example, a target could successfully keep some critical missing data from ever being found. Nevertheless, to help ensure the credibility of the rankings, care has been taken to avoid bloating the number of missing data tasks deemed critical for validation. Thus, Table 3.2 excludes future tasks, even quite important ones, such as securing vetting results for newly discovered direct evidence.

Considered from the standpoint of overall validation tasks, the dominant conventional (DC) view emerges as somewhat better off relative to its competitors than if inconsistencies alone are considered. As Table 3.3 shows, seven major validation tasks (dealing with six inconsistencies and one missing data task) are required for the DC view compared to six tasks for most of the other hypotheses. All are still considerably disadvantaged relative to the new recent challenge (NRC) view. Its overall requirements for validation are one to two critical missing data tasks. (Various views can improve their relative standing in the future, of course, by actually accomplishing validation tasks.)

When data stay missing: the denial issue

To be effective, a missing data test must provide for detecting denial. Assuming serious collection efforts are made, data that stay missing would

Table 3.2 Investigators' table: what are the most critical types of missing data for each hypothesis?

Hypotheses	DC	DN	OKC	OLC	R	NP	M	NRC
Critical missing data								
DKII2 (direct knowledgeable insider information)	yes	yes	yes	yes	yes	yes	yes	
O (observational data)			yes				yes	yes
DOC (documentary)		yes	yes	yes				
FA2 (feasibility assessment)							yes	yes?
XK2 (X's knowledge)					yes	yes		

Brief legend for posited hypotheses
DC: dominant conventional view (rely on evident protective measures for special capabilities); DN: do nothing substantial in peacetime but, in extremis, use special capabilities before they can be destroyed; OKC: compensate with other key (more secure and unknown to adversaries) capabilities; OLC: compensate with other lesser (more secure but known to adversaries) capabilities; R: use reinforcement to mitigate vulnerability; NP: use natural phenomena to mitigate vulnerability; M: surreptitiously provide for and move additional special capabilities in a crisis; NRC: new recent challenge view (rely on unexpected measures to prevent detection of some special capabilities and keep adversaries focused on evident protective measures).

generally indicate a hypothesis is invalid, since by definition important supporting data for an invalid hypothesis should not exist. But certain data that stay missing could be a sign of strength rather than weakness for a hypothesis, because they would suggest this is the truth a target is trying to hide—and the target simply has been successful at it thus far.

As indicated in Chapter 2, two checks can reduce this uncertainty. A hypothesis is more likely to be a victim of denial rather than invalid if it: (a) has fared well in the inconsistency test, which provides preliminary results on validity; and (b) the hypothesis has few missing data and they are not too diverse, because—as with deception—it would be difficult for a target to manipulate multiple, diverse data to enforce denial.[7] The two checks indicate NRC probably is a victim of denial rather than an invalid hypothesis. Given its lack of any inconsistencies, it is the strongest hypothesis to emerge from the inconsistency test. It also needs to secure only one to two missing data. And one of these is information from a feasibility test that is no real gauge of whether the hypothesis is or is not a victim of denial, since securing this information depends solely on whether the requisite U.S. technical analysis is performed. (As noted, the DC view only has one missing data item to secure. But this is hardly sufficient to indicate it is a victim of denial, given its very poor showing in the inconsistency test and earlier zero-based review.)

Table 3.3 Investigators' table: overall validation tasks to rank hypotheses[*]

Hypotheses	DC	DN	OKC	OLC	R	NP	M	NRC
Inconsistencies to rebut	6	4	4	4	4	4	3	0
Critical missing data to secure	1	2	3	2	2	2	3	1–2
Overall tasks for validation	**7**	**6**	**7**	**6**	**6**	**6**	**6**	**1–2**

Brief legend for posited hypotheses
DC: dominant conventional view (rely on evident protective measures for special capabilities); DN: do nothing substantial in peacetime but, in extremis, use special capabilities before they can be destroyed; OKC: compensate with other key (more secure and unknown to adversaries) capabilities; OLC: compensate with other lesser (more secure but known to adversaries) capabilities; R: use reinforcement to mitigate vulnerability; NP: use natural phenomena to mitigate vulnerability; M: surreptitiously provide for and move additional special capabilities in a crisis; NRC: new recent challenge view (rely on unexpected measures to prevent detection of some special capabilities and keep adversaries focused on evident protective measures).

Ranking: As a hypothesis accomplishes these tasks its status could improve. But for now NRC is clearly the strongest hypothesis, DC and OKC are generally the weakest, and five views are basically tied for a distant second place.

Note
[*] As the proffered hypothetical case shows, the methodology has various features that promote transparency. It provides a numerical basis for the ranking of hypotheses rather than settling for the more common but more ambiguous rankings, such as "possible," "probable," and "highly likely." The overall validation tasks themselves show the mix of assessed inconsistencies and critical missing data for each hypothesis. In addition, the inconsistency and missing data test charts can be readily consulted to see specifically with what body (or bodies) of data a given hypothesis is assessed to be inconsistent and what body (or bodies) of critical missing data it needs to secure. In each case, reference can then be made to the text accompanying these charts (as demonstrated for the missing data test) to see the detailed rationales for these specific judgments (see also Chapter 1, note 12).

Entries for the missing data chart

Critical missing data types in Table 3.2 cover direct knowledgeable insider information (DKII2); observational data (O); documentary data (DOC); feasibility assessment data (FA2); and data on X's knowledge (XK2). To avoid confusion with the DKII, FA, and XK entries in the inconsistency chart, DKII2, FA2, and XK2 are designated here for basically the same types of data. (Note: in the inconsistency test, XK data were confined to documentary information, but documentary information of course could apply more widely, as is intended with the DOC designation in the missing data test. Likewise, missing data bearing on X's knowledge, could come from various sources other than documents. Also, long known information [LKI] represents observational data and lax protective measures [LPM] are a special subset of such data. Again, observational data clearly have broader applications, as intended with the O designation in the missing data test. For a different intelligence issue, other types of data may be relevant. Moreover, the test on some issue might include specific categories of sensitive sources.)

Rationales for the missing data test assessments

Since the methodology presents a missing data test for the first time, detailing illustrative rationales for the specific judgments in its test chart (Table 3.2) is useful.

- Seven views need direct knowledgeable insider information (DKII2), particularly because they must compete with the new recent challenge (NRC) view that is backed by such direct evidence. Securing this direct evidence qualifies as a critical missing data task and is indicated as such in the chart. Although not included in the chart, a related and highly important task that qualifies at least as a future missing data task is to secure vetting results on any direct evidence that is found, to see if it is phony. DKII2 could be derived from either human or technical sources. Therefore, appropriate vetting, as my earlier Chapter indicated, could entail a polygraph exam or, as has applied for NRC, a risk assessment of compromise for the technical source. Then, as was the case for the direct evidence supporting NRC, the vetting results for DKII2 should be double-checked by comparing them with all other available data used in the inconsistency test. Depending on the outcome of the vetting and the double-check, the hypothesis backed by DKII2 may or may not improve its standing relative to other competing hypotheses. It is likely, in any event that, since NRC's evidence was found to be compatible with all other data, DKII2's support for another hypothesis would not enable that hypothesis to emerge as a close challenger to NRC.
- The other key capabilities (OKC), movement (M), and new recent challenge (NRC) views call for observational data (O) to help establish the basic existence of undetected capabilities or protective measures these hypotheses posit. In each case, O might still leave doubt all of them have been found.
- Documentary evidence (DOC) is desirable for all hypotheses but critical for the do nothing (DN) view, the other key capabilities (OKC) view and the other lesser capabilities (OLC) view. For DN, some evidence beyond the DKII2 data is required and the nature of this option makes it unlikely observational data could be found in peacetime. OKC and OLC compensate for vulnerability basically by helping to deter an adversary threat to the vulnerable capabilities and do not—in contrast, say, to the reinforcement (R) and natural phenomena (NP) views—purport to directly protect them. Thus, even if both OKC and OLC exist—a given for the posited OLC but in question for OKC—their link to protecting the vulnerable capabilities would still need to be established. Therefore, documentary support indicating X specifically has envisaged such a role for OKC or OLC is called for.

- The movement hypothesis (M) needs feasibility assessment data (FA2) that show it can overcome certain technical problems, noted by the investigators, to be a realistic option.
- In the inconsistency test chart (Table 3.1), feasibility data (FA) have been included in the information supporting the new recent challenge (NRC) view because, the investigators note, the data in hand do attest to the basic feasibility of the "unexpected measures." To definitively pin down such feasibility some possible additional effort (FA2), denoted with a question mark, is indicated.
- In the inconsistency chart data on X's knowledge (XK) are limited to X's awareness that the evident protective measures in LKI can be countered. XK2 refers to other situations where X's knowledge is a key issue, particularly whether X is aware its reliance instead on certain (standard) reinforcement measures (R) or protection by certain of its natural phenomena (NP) could also be countered. (The investigators note other well-established information indicates they can be.) If X's awareness were determined, the R and NP views could have a potential future task. They would need feasibility data (FA2) to see whether X could nevertheless have unique, workable and as yet undetected ways of using reinforcement or natural phenomena that would be effective. *A central objective of the overall methodology—which NRC's "unexpected measures" particularly exemplify—is to ensure analysts consider such "home grown" foreign actions that would be atypical for the U.S., or perhaps even irrational by its standards.*

Taking it from here

The overriding goal of the methodology is not modest. Simply put, it is to provide a more comprehensive and rigorous tool for conducting intelligence analysis, particularly threat analysis, than offered by other formal methodologies, or that the many and varied critiques of intelligence analysis over the years have suggested to remedy particular shortcomings that contribute to intelligence failures. But no tool is any good if it is too hard to use. This case study has been intended to show that although the methodology is ambitious—in both the problem areas it covers and the standards it tries to meet—it is nevertheless eminently doable.

The procedures illustrated in this hypothetical case, however, are not an inflexible set of guidelines. As analysts seek to apply them to particular threat issues they encounter, adjustments and refinements doubtless will be needed so the methodology can work best for them. In trying to implement the methodology, analysts should particularly consider two sources of help: they should have a software version developed and also look for insights and advice from outside reviewers with pertinent expertise.

Analysts will note that the hypothetical case study was put together without using a software package for the methodology, but such software should be relatively easy to develop. It would be roughly akin to the software version now available for Heuer's ACH methodology. This should greatly ease the chore of manipulating even larger numbers of hypotheses and data sets than used in this case study.

Outside reviewers can help analysts in various ways. As Chapter 2 argued, engaging a panel of outside experts can help legitimize the methodology—or something similar to it—as a norm that all views on a given threat have to meet. Politicizing interpretations of a threat would, therefore, become more difficult. Of even greater importance, however, is that, in contrast to the natural focus of post mortems on finding errors that led to failures to predict threats that have already happened, outside experts can be engaged to help analysts detect and correct a wide variety of errors in their ongoing analysis of a new threat—before such errors can have fateful consequences. In helping analysts implement the methodology better in these circumstances, outside experts might, for example, provide insights on certain collection that needs to be considered, relevant available data that should be included, additional assumptions that require examination and the like. In the context of such potential inputs, there is clearly a place for a reviewer to propose a new hypothesis that has not previously been considered. This should certainly be welcomed—but with the obvious and quite logical proviso that the new view should be subjected to the same overall testing process as any other hypothesis already being assessed by analysts.

Notes

1 Originally published by Karl Spielmann, "Using Enhanced Analytic Techniques for Threat Analysis: A Case Study Illustration," *International Journal of Intelligence and Counterintelligence*, vol. 27, no. 1, Spring 2014, pp. 132–155. Reprinted by permission of Taylor & Francis Ltd, www.tandfonline.com.
2 See Chapter 2.
3 A key finding of the National Commission on Terrorist Attacks Upon the United States (9/11 Commission) underscores the fact that the Intelligence Community's emphasis on better sharing of information to forestall future 9/11s is only a partial remedy. In commenting on the failure of the U.S. government to "connect the dots" and have any real appreciation of the suicide attacks being planned with commercial airplanes, the Commission flatly stated that: "the most important failure was one of imagination." See discussion of general findings in final *Report of the National Commission on Terrorist Attacks Upon the United States*, available on the website for the National Commission on Terrorist Attacks Upon the United States, archived on July 22, 2004: www.9-11commission.gov/report/911Report.pdf.

4 This hypothetical case study does not feature source references for two reasons: (1) the case is hypothetical, rather than a historically documented case; and (2) certain aspects of both the methodology and case study—such as the treatment of the pros and cons of using different types of intelligence data (e.g., direct vs. circumstantial evidence) are drawn from key lessons I learned, from dealing first hand as an analyst and manager with various threat cases over the years, particularly involving denial and deception (D&D) and alternative analysis issues. Unfortunately, these cases are not available for citation in an open article so that additional details or background on the analysis of the threats involved could not be provided to further illuminate the discussion.

5 As emphasized in Chapter 1, weighting can have a major impact on the integrity of any analysis that brings different bodies of data to bear to determine probability. An analyst has essentially two weighting options: try to assign different weights to the bodies of data or treat them as having equal weight. This choice affects statistical probability methods (see Chapter 4). It is also relevant for this methodology's efforts to rank hypotheses according to the number of validation tasks (to rebut assessed inconsistencies and secure critical missing data) each hypothesis has (see also Chapter 1, note 12). Deliberately assigning different weights is often attempted but is very hard to implement effectively. It has the worthy objective of ensuring that an "important" body of data appropriately counts more than a "less important" counterpart in determining the outcome of an analysis. But the relative importance of such bodies of data often will not be self-evident in the first place and how much weight the "important" one should actually be accorded will be even less obvious. Because of these large uncertainties, personal preferences in particular and sheer guesswork cannot help but influence how weights are assigned. As a result, the probability analysis will be quite subjective and falsely precise in quantitative terms. (The inability to tap performance records, which is an unfortunate drawback in intelligence analysis, increases this risk. Analysts cannot garner insights from analogous past cases to see how comparable bodies of data may have affected the results. See Chapter 1, notes 5 and 7.)

This methodology therefore opts for basically giving equal weight to all assessed inconsistencies and all critical missing data that constitute its validation tasks (with one exception, as elaborated in the missing data test discussion in the text). Equal weighting guards against making subjective judgments on the importance of a given body of data. It cannot, however, override the uncertainties inherent in weighting and firmly establish that all inconsistencies and missing data in fact have equal weight. Much more likely, equal weighting will undervalue some of them and overvalue some of them (although which ones will be affected and to what degree will remain indeterminate). Nevertheless, the impact of any distortions can be lessened, so that the basic integrity of the rankings is maintained.

If one has a substantial number of data sets to work with—which the methodology strongly urges analysts to strive for in any case—the chances are improved that those inconsistencies and missing data that are may be undervalued and those that may be overvalued will tend to balance out. This means that the ranking of the weakest hypotheses (with the most inconsistencies and missing data overall) will be least prone to distortion. But, by the same logic, the ranking of the strongest hypotheses (with the fewest of these validation task liabilities) will be most prone to distortion.

The hypothetical case shows, however, that distortions affecting the strongest hypotheses are not as serious as they may seem. The strongest hypothesis there has only 1–2 (i.e., 1.5) tasks but its nearest rivals have 6. For the strongest to lose first place, the net impact of any distortions would have to be implausibly severe. This suggests any distortion really worthy of an analyst's concern would be in the unlikely event of a close competition for first place—and with all competitors having very few validation tasks.

6 See note 4.

7 Denial can be a double-edged sword for intelligence analysts. If successful, it is a major obstacle to their getting at the truth. But it also can be an invaluable aid if reliably detected. What is being denied, after all, is the truth about some weapon capability, military plan, or whatever that the target does not want intelligence to find out. To the extent denial is effectively determined, therefore, it provides an important buttress for this proposed methodology's overall effort to rank hypotheses to see which is most likely to be correct.

By providing two checks to determine whether denial is at work, as discussed in the text, the methodology can be more reliable in detecting denial than other similar efforts. In particular, it avoids the risk of relying on apparent indicators that denial measures are being employed. As Chapter 2 has discussed, a security perimeter detected at some adversary facility may or may not be a real denial effort. It may be a ruse—in short, a deceptive use of denial—to divert intelligence collectors from the real secret. The standard wartime practice of "hiding" a dummy gun battery with camouflage offers the most vivid illustration of such deception. Since the dummy battery is pointless unless seen by the enemy, the camouflage is clearly not meant to be effective denial. The only function of the camouflage is to make the battery seem genuine, since the enemy would expect real batteries to have such protection.

Bibliography

Government Publishing Office, *Unclassified Version of the Report of the Commission on the Intelligence Capabilities of the United States Regarding Weapons of Mass Destruction*, March 31, 2005: www.gpo.gov/fdsys/pkg/GPO-WMD/pdf/GPO-WMD.pdf.

Heuer, Richards J., *Psychology of Intelligence Analysis*, Kindle ed., Center for the Study of Intelligence, Central Intelligence Agency, Washington, DC, 2016.

Heuer, Richards J. (with Randolph H. Pherson), *Structured Analytic Techniques for Intelligence Analysis*, 2nd ed., CQ Press, Los Angeles, 2014.

National Commission on Terrorist Attacks Upon the United States, *Report of the National Commission on Terrorist Attacks Upon the United States*, Final Report, July 22, 2004: www.9-11commission.gov/report/911Report.

Spielmann, Karl, "Strengthening Intelligence Threat Analysis," *International Journal of Intelligence and Counterintelligence*, vol. 25, no. 1, Spring 2012, pp. 19–43.

Spielmann, Karl, "Using Enhanced Analytic Techniques for Threat Analysis: A Case Study Illustration," *International Journal of Intelligence and Counterintelligence*, vol. 27, no. 1, Spring 2014, pp. 132–155.

4   I got algorithm

Can there be a Nate Silver in intelligence?[1]

Nate Silver is a prominent statistician/statistical probability analyst who, among other achievements, may be best known for making a very accurate prediction of President Obama's victory and the dimensions of it in the 2012 election.[2] In doing so, he probably redeemed (at least partially) the reputation of sophisticated mathematical modeling that was badly tarnished by its association with the poor investment decisions that brought us the financial debacle of 2008.[3] Does Silver have a potential counterpart in the intelligence business, where predicting the nature and likelihood of threats is a central concern, and what would that person have to do to rise to the occasion?

I have advanced a different approach to determining threat probability.[4] Nevertheless, in presenting my methodology on assessing and predicting threats, I have explicitly noted that analysts might well look to statistical probability analysis as another way to gain confidence that the particular hypothesis that they back on some threat is on target.

In any case, that statistical probability analysis secures a real foothold in all-source threat analysis may be only a matter of time, given significant technical advances in computing power. Prospects for exploiting "big data" are growing in many fields[5] and as public information alone makes clear, such exploitation is well under way in intelligence collection.

But my earlier work on these matters alerted me to some tough demands that any intelligence method needs to meet. Based on that work, I believe statistical probability analysis faces the following roadblocks.

Eight challenges for statistical probability analysis as a threat analysis tool

The demand for transparency

Both the strength and a central weakness of statistical probability analysis is that it is a job for real experts; especially, these days, computer and math wizards. The catch is that non experts, who would have to make life and death decisions based on it to deal with national security threats, cannot readily understand why they should believe it. Nor of course would the average citizen, who would have to be prepared to fully trust the experts if top decision makers, within the constraints of not divulging classified information, ventured to refer to such analysis to justify their decisions to the public.

To make this combination of transparency demands more concrete, consider the following hypothetical situation. Suppose that in early 2003, in the run up to the war in Iraq, an intelligence analyst carried out sophisticated mathematical modeling that showed an 82 percent probability for Iraq's possession of weapons of mass destruction (WMD). (Never mind that, within months, the failure to find WMD would reveal this analysis to have been woefully inaccurate.) Suppose further that, as then-Secretary of State Colin Powell was being provided with intelligence inputs for his now famous presentation of the U.S. case against Iraq, at the United Nations (UN) and before the world public, he was also given a detailed briefing on how this modeling was carried out.

How likely, in the first place, would Powell have found the modeling easy to understand and persuasive enough on its own to qualify as a major buttress for the U.S. case? And, if for some reason, he did try to explain the modeling to UN and TV audiences—so they would not have to take it on faith—would they have found it understandable enough to actually believe it? For both Secretary Powell and in his interaction with the public, the statistical probability analysis more likely would have been a hard sell.

So, overall, meeting the demand for transparency is a big—perhaps the biggest—challenge for any sophisticated mathematical modeling for intelligence, particularly threat analysis.

This was a big challenge as well for the methodology I advanced. As would statistical probability analysis, my suggested approach aims at being as precise as possible in its judgments on the probability of different views on the nature and likelihood of a given threat. It provides a numerical basis for ranking them, rather than settling for more common but more ambiguous qualitative judgments such as "possible," "probable" and the like.[6] But my method also tried to square this need to be precise with meeting the need to be as transparent as possible for non expert policy audiences. For example, it provides test charts that clearly show its judgments on the specific data support for each competing view and brief accompanying texts to provide the detailed rationales for those judgments.

Big data on intelligence performance: where is it?

Statistical probability analysis cannot be done in a vacuum. Like any other approach for intelligence analysis, it will be only as good as the data it uses. Indeed, even the most rudimentary probability exercises, like handicapping horse races, need to draw on something to make comparisons. That something is generally records. For the bookmaker, the records that matter are a horse's pedigree line, its performance over time, its response to different jockeys, its performance under different track conditions, and the like. Similar records are tapped for other horses in the race to allow for comparisons and enable odds to be set for the likelihood of each horse to win.

Statistical probability analysts would have a much tougher job judging the nature and likelihood of a looming threat. Performance records are meager for intelligence and are likely to remain so for security and bureaucratic reasons. Strictly speaking, judging intelligence performance is actually like judging how the bookmakers performed, not the horses. But this, of course, would be only one small step from asking how good were the records the bookmakers used, and how effectively they used them.

While major intelligence failures make the news, as does the role of the commissions that do the big post mortems to figure out why they occurred, statistical probability analysis would want to be able to draw on records that show both intelligence successes and failures. (Consider by analogy the absurdity of a bookmaker looking at only the races a horse has lost— and not also those it has won—in gauging its prospects for the next race.) Beyond this, the analysis would want to draw on more detailed breakdowns of such data on intelligence performance to see what insights can be applied to determine probability for the issue under current scrutiny.

Presumably, the analysis would start with asking: What past threats are similar to the current one—a tough question on its own? Moreover, which similar past threats did intelligence assess accurately and which did it fail to do so? And further, what factors seemed to make the difference between past successes and failures? For example, was a certain collection pivotal, or how well did analysts examine their underlying assumptions, or how effectively did they counter adversary efforts to deny intelligence critical information or deceive intelligence with phony facts? These and other questions would be necessary to glean insights from intelligence performance records that would, in effect, help analysts handicap different hypotheses on the nature and likelihood of a current threat.

To provide decent performance records for statistical probability analysis to draw on for judging any like cases in the future, intelligence organizations would have to do regular, detailed follow ups in the aftermath of individual threat assessments that they provide to policy-makers and military commanders, across a wide spectrum of cases. To my knowledge, except perhaps on a limited basis, such follow ups (in effect, "mini post mortems") have not been attempted—certainly not as a normal practice that provides appropriately broad and detailed coverage of intelligence cases.

To be useful, the mini post mortems would have to contain not only judgments on how these assessments actually fared in the real world— i.e., were they shown to be right or wrong?—but also the detailed break-downs on the factors affecting successes and failures discussed above. Even if the Intelligence Community (IC) signed on to make such performance records standard practice, compilation of decent records would take time. Meanwhile, statistical probability analysts would only have existing records to use, which would likely not have been set up to provide the kind of detailed data needed for making sound probability calculations. These records, though perhaps having some pockets of solid performance data, would also have many gaps. Almost certainly, key factors affecting past failures—and especially past successes, which have never been the subject of the big post mortems—would have received inadequate treatment. Overall, statistical probability analysts would be left to fill in the blanks with conjectures and surmises, a poor way to produce sound analysis. (These drawbacks, in fact, dissuaded me and other threat analysts over the years from relying on such records for judging threat probabilities.)

But the IC is unlikely, in any case, to start compiling decent records. Especially these days, detailed performance records would have the down-side of being a ticking time bomb for potential leakers. Beyond security concerns, compiling them would be bureaucratically onerous. Doing the mini post mortems, with the scope and level of detail for them to be most useful, would be a big chore. The process would be time consuming, dependent on real world feedback that often may be tardy or insufficient and, overall, give rise to various (and, sometimes, doubtless very heated) controversies.

In sum, while computer advances may hold promise for exploiting "big data" to further knowledge in many fields, this is not likely to happen for all-source threat analysis. The "big data" needed is unavailable and is likely to remain so. For statistical probability analysis, the lack of decent performance records is particularly serious. Statistical probability analysis is deprived of a standard underpinning, which usable records have long afforded it in the civilian world, for even making probability calculations for threat analysis. Thus, some suitable altern-ative would have to be found.

But what about other data, such as the information available on a given threat to compare different hypotheses as to their relative validity in judging the nature and likelihood of the threat? This is the data I had to figure out how to use to implement my own methodology for threat analysis. In putting the method together, I reasoned that—absent detailed intelligence performance records—the only sensible way to proceed was to pose the most basic intelligence questions possible: were analysts likely to differ on some threat issue? Except in rare cases, probably they would. (In any event, unless there were very solid grounds for unanimity, they should.) Was data necessary to sort out these differences? Unquestionably yes, on logical grounds alone. (And, if not, why engage in intelligence collection in the first place?) So, the pivotal question that emerged was simply: what is the best approach for using intelligence data as effectively as possible in order to find out which of various competing views on a threat is most likely to be correct?

There may be a number of ways to compare hypotheses, but I settled on determining data inconsistencies on a threat as the most prudent course of action: with no acceptable records to use, inconsistencies represent a metric for comparing hypotheses that is about as straightforward and universal as can be devised. Moreover, the use of inconsistencies has been tried and tested in methods popularized by the intelligence methodologist Richards Heuer and, before him, the prominent analyst of scientific method, Karl Popper. The basic rule of thumb is: the fewer inconsistencies a hypothesis has with relevant data (which makes establishing relevancy a key concern at the outset), the stronger claim it has to validity.

For threat analysis, the data demands for such hypothesis testing are especially stringent. My method had to make special efforts to ensure the quantity and quality of the bodies of data and, equally important, the soundness of the reasoning used to compare hypotheses. To be distinctive, statistical probability analysis presumably would not copy my method's emphasis on determining data inconsistencies. But whatever hypothesis testing it devises to conduct work on threat analysis given inadequate performance records, it would still face the same data demands.

Ensuring data quantity (1): don't overlook relevant available data

In addition to calling for better sharing of information, the 9/11 Commission emphasized that the main failing in averting the terrorist attacks was one of imagination.[7] To cope with this demand, my method urges using many hypotheses to stretch analysts' imagination on threat possibilities and reduce the risk that analysts will overlook some relevant available information. Using and testing many hypotheses pushes analysts to consider not only more threat possibilities but the relevant data to support them. Since a given hypothesis can only best its rivals if it has stronger data support, a given hypothesis will, or at least should, prompt an analyst to look for particular information that supports it. A statistical probability analysis should also be able to work with many hypotheses.

Testing only a few hypotheses, in fact, risks depriving an analyst of the ability to discover the truth. Even using many hypotheses cannot guarantee that the correct hypothesis—i.e., the one that captures the truth about some adversary course of action—is included among those being tested. Obviously the chance of this happening is greater, however, if more rather than fewer hypotheses are under scrutiny. (Testing many hypotheses, in fact, can improve threat analysis in various ways. Chapters 2 and 3 show at least seven ways it can help, some of them highlighted here.)

A statistical probability analyst would be tempted to suppose that brute computing power alone would do the job of bringing relevant data to light that would enable the making of probability judgments. After all, seeking data nuggets in masses of essentially raw data is a prominent collection activity these days—especially for intelligence professionals working in the area of terrorist threats, who look to computer power to help them assemble, correlate, and winnow large masses of such data. Elements of this activity have sparked public controversy over whether some of the data collected, particularly involving phone records, infringes on citizens' privacy rights.

But the need for considerable further analysis can be finessed only if the nuggets that emerge from even the most ambitious data mining operation contain truly compelling evidence: that is, evidence which is real "smoking gun" or "slam dunk" quality. This is evidence—from collection efforts of any sort—that can pretty much stand alone, with little or no massaging from all-source analysts, in conveying accurate warning or other vital insights to decision makers. In general, however, collectors only occasionally obtain such truly compelling evidence. Any less compelling data needs to be fed into an analytic process of hypothesis testing, using these items and others to see how they help determine the nature and likelihood of a given threat. A central aim of using many hypotheses is to try to ensure that the analyst is sensitized to appreciate the relevance of as many of these bodies of information as possible for this analysis.

Again, the work of the statistical probability analyst would be eased in bringing as much relevant data to bear as possible, if the analyst could also access the appropriate detailed intelligence performance records. Compared to searches of masses of essentially raw data, the relevant data for assessing threats from various quarters should be more discernible in such records. But, as earlier discussed, in contrast to many civilian issues, statistical probability analysts cannot count on the availability of this resource.

Ensuring data quantity (2): don't slight data on adversary "irrationality"

Any methodology for threat analysis, aspiring to include a respectable amount of scientific rigor and objectivity, must figure out how to accommodate foreign behavior that does not play by its rules. This requirement was driven home to me not only by the example of suicide attacks, such as 9/11 (now reinforced by other extreme murderous acts by terrorists), but also by numerous instances of adversaries whose home grown techniques for solving technical problems in developing weapon capabilities of all sizes would be atypical for the U.S. Overall, paying due regard to "irrational" adversary behavior—whether it is really irrational by almost any standard or simply different and unfamiliar—however it might manifest itself in various aspects of a threat is important (see also Chapter 1, notes 8, 15, and 17).

The need to deal with real or seeming irrationality places a premium on tapping the expertise of country or regional experts in devising hypotheses to be tested. They are the most likely to have the requisite insights to ensure that hypotheses about adversary courses of action that seem implausible by U.S. or Western standards—and the data to support them—are appropriately represented among the tested hypotheses.

Using many hypotheses for testing generally facilitates taking "irrational" adversary behavior into account. Otherwise, if only a few hypotheses are tested and the insights of the aforementioned experts are not considered, a substantial risk develops that foreign behavior out of sync with U.S. or Western expectations will fail to make the cut for hypothesis testing.

Furthermore, using multiple hypotheses for testing helps guard against giving undue deference or weight to the view of a given country or regional expert on an adversary's "irrational" behavior. Experts with roughly the same credentials can, of course, still differ about an adversary's mindset and actions. During the Cold War, for example, experts all claiming to be able to "think Soviet" often had markedly different views on what the Soviets were up to, often on the same issue. So, when differences among these experts emerge, subjecting all of them to a process of hypothesis testing seems only sensible.

Some scholars see country or regional expertise as having characteristics (such as empathy for the peculiarities of a foreign culture) not easily captured by scientific method. But, as long as these experts are required to back up their views with data, that should not be a problem. Using many hypotheses for testing calls for providing relevant data (whatever its origin) to support each view and then seeing how all the data ultimately sorts out. Thus, country or regional expertise can be taken into account while holding it to appropriate standards of scientific rigor and objectivity. A statistical probability analysis should be able to deal with this concern also.

Another data issue, though, appears to be tougher for statistical probability analysis to address. It involves the importance of missing data as a gauge of the relative validity of a hypothesis. In my method, the final ranking of hypotheses is based on a tally of both the assessed inconsistencies that a hypothesis has to rebut and the critical missing data it needs to secure. Missing data is, in fact, both a data quantity issue (i.e., don't ignore it) and a data quality issue (i.e., don't misjudge its significance). Can statistical probability analysis accommodate missing data as a factor in its calculations? Frankly, I do not know but my sense is that this is not normally what the analysis is geared to address. But it is first necessary to highlight another data quality problem that matters—phony data.

Ensuring data quality (1): the challenge of foreign deception

No statistical probability analysis wants to rely on phony data but could easily do so if it does not provide for dealing with foreign deception which, though generally not an academic concern, can wreak havoc for intelligence analysis. This matter can be tackled in a way that provides an independent means to double-check the vetting of not only human but also technical sources. In the case of technical sources, vetting calls for particular collectors to make a risk assessment of whether the foreign target could be aware of the collection and thus try to use it to feed the U.S. phony information. Any statistical probability analysis should take steps therefore to get a handle on the danger of deception for data it is using from both types of sources.

Given the controversy in recent years over the effectiveness of "hard" vs. "soft" interrogation methods for vetting human sources, it is important to appreciate that vetting per se is not infallible. Seeing no need to take sides in the controversy, my method thus proceeds on the premise that independent double-checking of the vetting simply makes sense. On a given intelligence issue, the method focuses on determining whether the information provided is at odds with other, diverse information that has been brought to bear for conducting an inconsistency test to compare hypotheses. If so, the data from the source is likely to be deceptive (and this same procedure applies for technical source information). However the human source vetting may have been carried out, such independent double-checking seems merely prudent.

Ensuring data quality (2): the challenge of foreign denial

Dealing with the deception issue also underscores the importance of linking up the treatment of deception with efforts to both identify and interpret missing data because, again, unlike in academe, foreign denial is a special challenge for intelligence analysis. Even if statistical probability analysis somehow accommodates missing data in the data it uses to compare the likelihood of different views on a threat, missing data can signify different things. Some can point to an invalid hypothesis, since, by definition, an invalid hypothesis should be missing important supporting data (see also, Chapter 2, note 16). But some missing data can indicate a valid hypothesis for which the data exist but are being deliberately denied to intelligence by the adversary.

To make matters worse, a statistical probability analysis will have to cope with the problem, which my method seeks to do, that analysts can be deliberately misled by the adversary about whether denial is actually occurring. For example, analysts might assume a security perimeter that collection detects at an adversary facility is a sure sign of a significant military capability being hidden there, that its existence is being denied to intelligence. If so, this information would help validate some hypothesis that posits such a capability, perhaps even at that location. But what if the adversary actually intended for intelligence to detect the security perimeter? Its goal would be to divert the collector from the real secret, which may be that the military capability is at a different place or doesn't exist at all. This would qualify as a deception—to be precise, the deceptive use of apparent denial measures. Thus, the information collected on the security perimeter would not underpin a valid hypothesis about what the adversary was up to. It would simply lend credence to, perhaps even make the case for, an invalid hypothesis about the adversary's behavior.

To enable analysts to avoid being so dependent on such problematic information, which they might commonly confront in one form or another in identifying and assessing foreign threats, my method lays out different procedures for determining denial. They combine two gauges: (a) how a given hypothesis fared in previous inconsistency testing (this testing provides a preliminary judgment on its validity); and (b) the number and diversity of data deemed missing. (Few and not so diverse is a good sign that denial is being employed, because multiple, diverse data would be hard for an adversary to manipulate).

In sum, unless a statistical probability analysis deals with the denial issue, in some manner at least roughly similar to what I have attempted, it will be distorting its inclusion of missing data—using it willy-nilly to either buttress or detract from the overall data support required for particular hypotheses. And, if, in order to skirt the denial issue, it opts to omit missing data as a factor affecting the strength or weakness of a given hypothesis, it would simply be cherry-picking the data that it deems worthy for its calculations, which would be no less of a distortion.

While denial and deception (D&D) represent the damage that foreign adversaries inflict on intelligence analysis, an equally serious problem is that analysts can also distort analysis by fooling themselves. The general remedy for this self-inflicted wound from cognitive biases is for analysts to place a priority on examining the assumptions underlying a given analysis. But two types of faulty assumptions (concerning consistency and weighting data) constitute especially harmful bad thinking and require special remedial measures.

Dealing with bad thinking (1): the challenge of consistency–inconsistency determinations

In one way or another, statistical probability analysis will have to deal with determinations of consistency and inconsistency in the data it uses for its probability calculations. The analysis presumably would rest its overall judgments, on the probability of different hypotheses, on other grounds than these determinations which are the main metric in my method.

The particular way statistical probability calculations might be applied, however, is beyond the scope of this book and my competence. Indeed, given poor performance records, statistical probability analysts themselves might have to be innovative. Still, as part of its handling of data, any statistical probability analysis, however sophisticated, would confront consistency–inconsistency issues. Some would not be too difficult, and any statistical probability analysis would doubtless handle them well. For example, in calculating the probability of some course of action by an adversary, analysts would avoid using data to support a given hypothesis that was inconsistent with what the hypothesis posits about an adversary's behavior. But this is only part of the problem.

Data consistent with a given hypothesis can also be consistent with other hypotheses. Unless a statistical probability analysis is attentive to determining whether consistency of a body of data with a given hypothesis is shared with other hypotheses, judgments on the likelihood of an adversary's course of action can be seriously distorted. The post mortem, by the National Commission on the Intelligence Capabilities of the United States

Regarding Weapons of Mass Destruction (the WMD Commission), on the intelligence failure on Iraqi WMD specifically identified this misplaced confidence in consistency as an egregious example of poor analytic trade-craft.[8] This faulty assumption was hardly a minor glitch; it contributed to erroneous intelligence judgments with enormous real world consequences.

To deal with the problem of an analyst's misplaced confidence in consistency, my method provides a shared consistency test to examine whether plausible circumstances exist in which data supporting one hypothesis on a threat, particularly the dominant view, could also be consistent with other views. Failing to use some procedure like the shared consistency test can lead statistical probability analysis to give undue weight to the data supporting one potential course of action while omitting deserved data support for one or more competing views, thereby distorting the analysis.

Dealing with bad thinking (2): the overarching challenge of weighting data

Any analysis that uses more than one body of data must determine whether different bodies of data should be accorded the same weight or different weights. This is not just some "down in the weeds" issue that only methodologists would fuss about. Indeed, ongoing public debate over the payoff of certain controversial interrogation methods vividly illustrates that even "weighting" practices sometimes make the news. In the context of various other information relevant to some threat that was averted, how can a sound judgment be made regarding the importance of the information gained by such methods? Was the information pivotal or merely ancillary in staving off the danger? So weighting is, first of all, a tough problem that clearly matters for intelligence. Moreover, weighting is a particularly nasty problem, because analysts confront pitfalls wherever they turn. They can wrongly assume that reliably assigning different weights to different bodies of data is possible. They can also wrongly assume that simply relying on equal weighting is a safe fallback.

As to the first assumption, to assign different weights unless one has very good background information is highly risky. If statistical probability analysts could draw on detailed intelligence performance records, for example, they might be in a position to identify the types of data that had a greater or lesser determining role in assessments of previous threats similar to the one currently being assessed. Absent detailed intelligence performance records, however, deliberately assigning different weights faces considerable uncertainty, not only about the relative importance of different bodies of data but about how much more important a given body of data may be compared to another. Weighting heavily shaped by personal preferences and sheer guesswork can easily result.

As to the second assumption, equal weighting obviously guards against playing favorites but on its own can also distort analysis. In reality, except in rare cases, different bodies of data are unlikely to have an equal impact in securing an accurate assessment of some issue. They are likely to have different impacts. The catch is that, by and large, analysts have no reliable way of knowing what the real differences in impact might be. (If so, they could of course take a decent stab at deliberately assigning weights.) Unfortunately, for most analysts this issue never comes up on their radar, since they don't much ponder weighting issues in the first place. As a result, they routinely proceed with analyses that simply treat all bodies of data as equals by default.

My method tries to steer clear of both types of faulty assumptions. As would statistical probability analysis, it aims to rank hypotheses on a numerical basis, placing a premium on avoiding subjective judgments and false precision in making such rankings. Therefore, absent detailed intelligence performance records, my method could not responsibly try to assign different weights to the bodies of data used in a given assessment. Because of the uncertainties involved, doing so would likely seriously distort its judgments on the relative strengths and weaknesses of the hypotheses being tested. But, in opting for equal weighting, the method also makes a special effort to remedy its major shortcoming: by its nature, equal weighting will tend to overvalue some bodies of data and undervalue others. The key remedy is to use as many bodies of relevant data as possible—which the testing of many hypotheses helps secure. This increases the chances that those bodies of data that may be overvalued and those that may be undervalued will tend to balance out, thereby minimizing potential distortion of how hypotheses stand in the rankings (see also Chapter 1, note 7).

Statistical probability analysts would have to grapple with these same weighting issues in making their own quantitative probability judgments for threat analysis. Moreover, because weighting affects the basic integrity and soundness of an analysis, policymakers should be given an explicit and clear explanation of how weighting was handled.

Judging the prospects for statistical probability analysis as a threat analysis tool

In light of the eight challenges, can any aspiring Nate Silver find a comfortable home in the intelligence business? Statistical probability analysis probably can find ways to deal with or work around many of these challenges. Because it may be novel for statistical probability analyses to include—and because it is bound up with the denial issue—missing data may be one of the truly tough challenges. Two, however, appear to be basically intractable: the need for transparency and the inadequacy of intelligence performance records. Given the breakthroughs computers have been making in all sorts of areas, to some this judgment may seem too bleak. But is it?

Advances in computing power do hold promise for statistical probability analysis as a threat analysis tool, particularly in two ways: (1) they enable data to be processed quickly, and (2) they enable the processing of truly enormous amounts of data (popularly known these days as "big data").[9] Rapid data processing would greatly facilitate providing timely warning to national security decision makers—one of their most crucial intelligence needs. Processing large quantities of data would greatly facilitate exploitation of any relevant voluminous records, increasing the chances of discovering patterns, trends, and the like in the data that would, in turn, improve the accuracy of current threat assessments.

But timely warning, to be useful, depend on non expert decision makers readily comprehending and believing the warning that rapid processing of data would provide them. And improving the accuracy of current threat assessments by exploiting relevant voluminous records depends on such records (and not just collations of essentially raw data) being available. Statistical probability analysis seems unlikely to satisfy either of these conditions.

My method makes special efforts to ensure transparency by providing test charts displaying data support for particular hypotheses and appropriate easily understood backup for them. Transparency is greatly aided, moreover, by the fact that the math is very simple—no complex algorithms are involved. As for meeting warning needs, the method does not look to fast data processing to achieve timely warning, although appropriate software could speed up the data handling the method calls for. Mainly, the method addresses warning needs by providing interim judgments as its testing process proceeds, affording decision makers early warning inputs before testing is completed. Unfortunately, the method has had to make do without detailed intelligence performance records.

Transparency will be a much more vexing problem for statistical probability analysis, precisely because of its dependency on mathematical calculations that require expertise. Mathematical calculations are the defining characteristic of statistical probability analysis, whether it uses centuries-old Bayesian probability methods or the more modern computer-assisted modeling techniques. Statistical probability analysts would, of course, first have to make the bodies of data and reasoning they use comprehensible, so that non expert policymakers find the under-pinnings of the analysis to be credible. But, above all, these analysts would have to make the resulting calculations easily understood—a deed likely to be especially difficult.

So is transparency really an intractable challenge? Until some technical or other breakthrough occurs that would make non experts comfortable with statistical probability analysis, it certainly seems so. As a non expert, I have no recommendations for simplifying the math—if that is at all possible. But statistical probability analysts need to make serious efforts to do so or, as an intended threat analysis tool, their analysis will from the outset be met with skepticism from key national security customers. In fact, in dealing with national security threats, top decision makers will be reluctant to rely on an intelligence input that they cannot readily understand for a combination of reasons: the life and death consequences of the decisions they might have to make based on it; their ultimate responsibility to defend their decisions to the average citizen; and the likelihood that they would at least have a general awareness that sophisticated mathematical modeling has had a mixed record in the civilian world.

As for whether the challenge of inadequate intelligence performance records—that would keep the promise of exploiting big intelligence data from being realized—is really intractable, there is nothing to suggest other-wise. Serious concerns about leaks and bureaucratic equities make the compilation of appropriately broad and detailed performance records a remote prospect. And, if the IC did start compiling them, they would not be complete enough for many years ahead to be sufficiently useful.

The lack of such records for statistical probability analysis, moreover, is not just a matter of missing something that would be "nice to have." Without recourse to usable records—which have long been a standard underpinning for conducting probability calculations in the civilian world—finding a suitable alternative would be necessary for addressing threat issues. Though securing decent records may be intractable, finding a fallback for statistical probability calculations may not be. In any case, knowledgeable statistical probability analysts, fully conversant with the techniques available to their discipline, should be able to judge whether this assumption is optimistic.

Because the choice of an approach can obviously determine whether sound probability calculations get made, what statistical probability profes-sionals settle on when decent records are lacking is a critical decision. It is all the more important since what is involved is not the chance to get it right in betting on sporting events, or forecasting winners in elections, or selecting stocks to buy. In threat analysis, what is at stake is whether one can help predict foreign developments that are dangers to the country.

The heart of the matter: improving intelligence prediction

Although predicting is difficult because of the many uncertainties it confronts, intelligence organizations do not have the luxury of avoiding the making of predictions. Policymakers want professional help in getting a heads up on threats or other international developments affecting the security or other interests of the country. To meet this demand, dealing in some manner with the uncertainties affecting prediction—and not ducking the problem—is the only responsible recourse for the IC in general and for individual analysts.

Statistical probability analysis purports to offer, above all, a method for making predictions. Therefore, in gauging its potential role as a threat analysis tool, the critical question is ultimately whether it can do a better job at making predictions than approaches already available to intelligence, particularly, standard IC estimate practices and the approach I have offered for assessing threat probability.

How IC estimates handle prediction: reflecting group consensus. Estimates have authority because they reflect the collective judgments of the IC's many component organizations. This collective authority is invoked, for example, when, for a given judgment presented to policymakers, estimates commonly state that the IC has "high" or some other level of confidence in it. Despite seeming to work well for the most part, by its nature such a collegial process for making predictions has a significant drawback: it tends to come down on the side of conventional wisdom about the threat or other issue being considered (see also Chapter 1, pp. 17–18).

The estimate process makes specific allowance for individual agencies to register dissenting views, but this does not go far enough. Dissenting views and the dominant view they challenge are not normally subjected to a decisive contest, which the challenger might, from time to time, have some chance to win. In my experience in working many estimates, I was aware of no estimate where a dissenting view wound up supplanting the reigning dominant view as the IC's official position. My experience may be exceptional, but I doubt it. Analysts might do well to research the decades-long estimates record to see if dissents ever have won out.

These estimate practices are also deficient in the area that is a major sticking point for statistical probability analysis—transparency. Even if the standard invocation that the IC has some level of confidence in a particular judgment is well founded, it still begs for an up front, detailed recitation of the reasons why. Policymakers should be able to knowledgeably decide on their own whether they share that confidence, rather than basically defer to the IC's authority. Likewise, when IC estimates fail to engage a dissenting view in a decisive contest with the reigning dominant view, how is the policymaker supposed to be able to knowledgeably judge which view to believe?

Hypothesis testing: an alternative approach to prediction. My method and statistical probability analysis offer hypothesis testing as a basic alternative to the IC's collegial approach. Both provide a level playing field for competing views and closely compare them to establish their relative probability. My method also promotes transparency. All three approaches have different expectations and criteria for tackling prediction.

As laid out in Chapter 1's discussion of the logic of intelligence analysis and its challenges, my method contends that improving threat prediction calls for a new look, focused on not making the prediction problem worse. This new look—underlying all of the techniques in my method—argues the following: uncertainties already make the prediction problem bad enough, because they risk making predictions inaccurate. By their nature, whether uncertainties will ultimately undercut a given prediction, break in its favor, or have little or no effect on it is difficult to pin down beforehand. Thus, uncertainties can be faulted for risking inaccuracy, but not for predetermining it. But if predictions are based on analyses with significant flaws, this risk of inaccuracy can be seriously compounded. A badly flawed analysis virtually ensures a wrong prediction.

By taking some practical measures before predictions are made, however, the flaws that are sources of error can largely be remedied. In contrast, effectively reducing uncertainties, making them less likely to undercut a prediction, is a much tougher task. Indeed, even identifying the relevant uncertainties in a given case is a big challenge. Past successful predictions doubtless faced similar uncertainty issues and either somehow overcame them or, as my method seeks to do, worked around them. But without detailed records on intelligence successes, useful lessons are unavailable.

The upshot is that, although analysts should seize any sensible opportunity to reduce uncertainties, concentrating on analytic flaws offers the more realistic prospect for substantially improving prediction. This is because: (1) compared to uncertainties, analytic flaws are more likely to be detrimental to prediction (fortunately, by their nature, uncertainties only sometimes undercut predictions); and (2) analytic flaws are also likely to be easier to fix, since analysts have more control over them. While even identifying relevant uncertainties can be hard, my method pinpoints a range of fixable flaws for analysts to look out for.

All of this suggests that the standard guidance for improving prediction—namely, to focus on "managing uncertainties"—shortchanges analysts. It sets the wrong priority by slighting the damage from analytic flaws and seems too difficult to implement to be practical. Instead of trying to manage uncertainties to somehow reduce their negative impact on predictions, seeking to contain their negative impact by managing analytic flaws makes more sense. These flaws, as noted, can seriously compound the risk of inaccuracy that uncertainties pose. To underscore that this containment approach is practical, a case study illustrates my methodology—which proponents of managing uncertainties should try to emulate—and demonstrates in detail how analytic flaws can be managed.

In fact, managing analytic flaws to avoid making the prediction problem worse can be boiled down to simple, actionable guidance for analysts: before making predictions, minimize errors from analytic flaws. In other words, follow the standard that the Hippocratic Oath sets for physicians: "First, do no harm."

Both IC estimates and statistical probability analysis give insufficient attention to the impact of analytic flaws, which are likely to be especially troublesome with modern threats. For the IC to rely on conventional wisdom to predict particular threats even in the relatively defined threat context of the Cold War was risky. But relying on conventional wisdom is riskier in today's more fluid and less well understood threat environment. With rapidly evolving modern threats, any conventional wisdom that comes into fashion is likely to be more tenuous and error prone. For its part, statistical probability analysis risks placing too much faith in technology to override analytic flaws, and even uncertainties, that can cause errors in predicting modern threats.

Conventional wisdom is, in any case, susceptible to flaws resulting from sources of error that could have been dealt with because, by its nature, it is widely accepted and not questioned much—especially if endorsed by many smart people. Conventional wisdom can sometimes, perhaps even often, make accurate predictions. Nonetheless, prediction is bound to be improved when alternative views get a real chance to compete and they and the dominant view are all intensely scrutinized for significant flaws. This, of course, is what hypothesis testing calls for.

Consequently, the basic question for the IC is whether it can incorporate hypothesis testing in its estimate process and become less reliant on conventional wisdom—which is expressed as a group consensus that Chapter 1 extensively critiques[10]—to make predictions. For decades however, collegial authority, expressed by a vote, has determined the IC's official position. Hypothesis testing obviously would require a test, not a vote, to be the real determinant. For decades, mainstream views have of course been scrubbed, but not to the point of letting real competitors emerge. Dissents have had a slim chance at best of becoming more than just footnotes to a mainstream view. Given these strong conservative forces, adopting hypothesis testing seems highly unlikely for the IC, unless it is mandated as part of some overall top-level IC reform.

For now, analysts will have to chip away at the problem, and my methodology can aid them. As the first major stage of testing in my method, I have proposed (and demonstrated) a zero-based review to help hypothesis testing get a hearing when entrenched dominant views obstruct it. This review provides a rigorous evaluation of a dominant view's data support and reasoning. In an estimate context, a dominant view's backers would expect that view to be voted the official position, which the IC would then have to stand behind and defend. These backers, therefore, would have no legitimate grounds to object to this thorough scrub. The dominant view might or might not pass muster (see Chapter 1, note 10). If significant shortcomings are revealed, a strong *prima facie* case for additional views to be considered would develop and all views closely compared. In short, a zero-based review would force the issue for hypothesis testing to be carried out, and thus help the IC avoid making the prediction problem worse.

Hypothesis testing for estimates would have the advantage of being able to tap the collective brain power of the IC's many member organizations to generate many hypotheses and refine the testing. Hypothesis testing can also promote transparency and defang the politicization problem, since no view on a threat (even if favored by certain powerful interests) could evade this test.

In the long term, a major implication for the IC of adopting hypothesis testing (whether my method or something similar) is that it could provide a natural transition for estimates from intelligence practices nurtured during the Cold War to those more in tune with the digital age. Statistical probability analysis, after all, has its own brand of hypothesis testing and could well become a future tool for estimates. Indeed, many of its analysts may have high expectations that, with continuing technical advances, computer-assisted mathematical modeling is ready made for such intelligence prediction. For them, the simple avoidance of making the prediction problem worse is likely to seem too restrictive as a goal. Why not hold out the prospect of reducing uncertainties enough to achieve near certainty in predictions?

Before anything close to near certainty is attainable, however, the challenges for statistical probability analysis would have to be satisfactorily addressed. Given inadequate intelligence performance records, the first challenge is to ensure that an alternative underpinning for making statistical probability calculations is sound and not error prone. Moreover, the analysis would have to deal with the challenges inherent in ensuring the quantity and quality of data and avoiding faulty assumptions. They all involve sources of error that need to be remedied. If these challenges are slighted or ignored, pushing ahead with sophisticated mathematical modeling would not bring more intelligence successes. Doing so would only make the prediction problem worse. Thus, even though it has the merit of using hypothesis testing—and might promise much in time—statistical probability analysis has serious work to do before it can reliably improve threat prediction.

Are practical steps enough to improve prediction or is computer help needed?

Already available in published articles, my method's hypothesis testing can help analysts improve threat prediction. It offers practical steps in managing analytic flaws that compound the risk of inaccuracy that uncertainties pose—flaws that are sources of error and make the prediction problem worse. Since analysts work to give policymakers a heads up, abiding by the standard of "first, do no harm" comes down to pursuing one overall task: before making predictions, minimize errors from analytic flaws.

As they apply the method, analysts should be alert to additional flaws that are sources of error and devise their own remedies. Since uncertainties cannot be wished away, the method indicates the practical limits to what any analyst can reasonably be expected to accomplish, limitations which should be made clear to policymakers.

Where does that leave statistical probability analysis? To offer the equivalent of what my method offers, it must successfully address seven of the eight challenges. (Both approaches simply must acknowledge the lack of intelligence performance data.) But even if the challenges are met, to make a unique contribution, statistical probability analysis would have to achieve more.

To indicate where statistical probability analysis might provide added value, a look at some critical problem areas is instructive. My method says the following about where it can offer no guarantees, given the persistence of uncertainties, but still make real improvements:

- *When hypotheses are underrepresented* the method says: testing many hypotheses cannot guarantee that the correct hypothesis—the one that actually reflects what the adversary is up to—is included among them, but it can improve the chances that it is.
- *When foreign deception occurs* the method says: independently double-checking the vetting of a source (sources) cannot guarantee a sophisticated deception will be unable to slip through the cracks, but it can improve the chances that a deception will be detected.

- *When foreign denial occurs* the method says: since "one doesn't know what one doesn't know," no guarantee is available that an analyst will realize some important data on a threat issue is missing, but the chances are improved if a serious attempt is made to identify and seek out missing data.
- *When cognitive biases muddle analyst thinking* the method says: there can be no guarantee an analyst will avoid making faulty assumptions that distort analysis, but the chances are improved if examining one's assumptions is a priority.

The implication is that statistical probability analysis must set its sights high to make a real contribution to threat prediction. For example, where my method says uncertainties make any guarantees of overcoming various problem areas impossible, statistical probability analysts could try to show that their analyses could still reduce uncertainties enough to come close to offering guarantees. In effect, this means aiming for near certainty in threat prediction.

But is achieving near certainty in threat prediction feasible? From a technical standpoint, I do not know. What I do know, however, is that achieving such a lofty goal is not just a matter of making advances in computing capabilities and having the know how to devise complex algorithms for effectively exploiting those capabilities. The basic message here is that any potential Nate Silvers must grapple with an entire set of other issues in order to have a solid foundation for applying statistical probability analysis to threats—whatever goals may be set for prediction. As I found out in devising my own methodology, this involves taking on a range of difficult, substantive problems that affect the quantity and quality of data and the soundness of the reasoning that are brought to bear on threat issues. How effectively analysts deal with these problems—whether they are aided by computers or not—can spell the difference between accuracy and error in what they provide to policymakers seeking to keep the country safe.

Notes

1 Originally published by Karl Spielmann, "I Got Algorithm: Can There Be a Nate Silver in Intelligence?" *International Journal of Intelligence and Counterintelligence*, vol. 29, no. 3, Fall 2016, pp. 525–544. Reprinted by permission of Taylor & Francis Ltd, www.tandfonline.com.
2 I make personal reference to Mr Silver to hold him up as a kind of model for intelligence analysts, because of his reputation as a basically successful prognosticator versed in modern techniques of statistical probability analysis. (Note: this chapter (as originally published) was written before the results of the 2016

election were known and Mr Silver, among many others, did not accurately predict those results.) See also, Chapter 1, note 19.

3 See also Chapter 1, note 16.

4 See Chapters 2 and 3, which were originally published as: "Strengthening Intelligence Threat Analysis," *International Journal of Intelligence and Counterintelligence*, vol. 25, no. 1, Spring 2012 and "Using Enhanced Analytic Techniques for Threat Analysis: A Case Study Illustration," *International Journal of Intelligence and Counterintelligence*, vol. 27, no. 1, Spring 2014, pp. 132–155.

5 For a discussion of the many potential applications of advances in computing power—particularly in various traditional academic disciplines—for extracting valuable insights from large masses of data, see Jonathan Shaw, "Why 'Big Data' Is a Big Deal," *Harvard Magazine*, vol. 116, no. 4, March–April 2014, pp. 30–35.

6 See Chapter 1, note 12.

7 In commenting on the failure of the U.S. government to "connect the dots" and have any real appreciation of the suicide attacks being planned with commercial airplanes, the 9/11 Commission flatly stated that: "the most important failure was one of imagination." See discussion of general findings in the final *Report of the National Commission on Terrorist Attacks Upon the United States*, available on website for the National Commission on Terrorist Attacks Upon the United States, archived on July 22, 2004.

8 The WMD Commission report, dealing with the intelligence failure on Iraqi WMD, specifically identified the cognitive bias problem of analysts having a misplaced confidence in the consistency of their view with key data: "When we reviewed finished intelligence, we found egregious examples of poor tradecraft, such as using a piece of evidence to support an argument when the same piece supported exactly the opposite argument—and failing to note that fact." See Internet site, Government Publishing Office, *Unclassified Version of the Report of the Commission on the Intelligence Capabilities of the United States Regarding Weapons of Mass Destruction*, March 31, 2005: www.gpo.gov/fdsys/pkg/GPO-WMD/pdf/GPO-WMD.pdf, p. 408.

9 While trying to take into account the impact of computer advances, this book does not attempt to tackle the problem of analyzing cyber threats, which is a huge issue in its own right. (For a useful overview, see: Martin Rudner, "Cyber-Threats to Critical National Infrastructure: An Intelligence Challenge," *International Journal of Intelligence and Counterintelligence*, vol. 26, no. 3, 2013, pp. 453–481). Nevertheless, as with the discipline of statistical probability analysis, I believe my method also has similar useful lessons for the intelligence field of cyber threat analysis. This is particularly so, since cyber threats embody a big new version of the longstanding challenge from foreign D&D, which my method addresses.

10 See esp. Chapter 1, p. 20.

Bibliography

Brown, Anthony Cave, *Bodyguard of Lies*, Harper & Row, New York, 1975.

Government Publishing Office, *Unclassified Version of the Report of the Commission on the Intelligence Capabilities of the United States Regarding Weapons of Mass Destruction*, March 31, 2005: www.gpo.gov/fdsys/pkg/GPO-WMD/pdf/GPO-WMD.pdf.

Heuer, Richards J., *Psychology of Intelligence Analysis*, Kindle ed., Center for the Study of Intelligence, Central Intelligence Agency, Washington, DC, 2016.

Heuer, Richards J. (with Randolph H. Pherson), *Structured Analytic Techniques for Intelligence Analysis*, 2nd ed., CQ Press, Los Angeles, 2014.

Kahneman, Daniel, *Thinking, Fast and Slow*, Farrar, Straus & Giroux, New York, 2011.

National Commission on Terrorist Attacks Upon the United States, *Report of the National Commission on Terrorist Attacks Upon the United States*, Final Report, July 22, 2004: www.9-11commission.gov/report/911Report.pdf.

Rudner, Martin, "Cyber-Threats to Critical National Infrastructure: An Intelligence Challenge," *International Journal of Intelligence and Counterintelligence*, vol. 26, no. 3, September 2013, pp. 453–481.

Shaw, Jonathan, "Why 'Big Data' Is a Big Deal," *Harvard Magazine*, vol. 116, no. 4, March–April 2014, pp. 30–35.

Silver, Nathan, *The Signal and the Noise: Why So Many Predictions Fail—But Some Don't*, Penguin Books, New York, 2012.

Spielmann, Karl, "Strengthening Intelligence Threat Analysis," *International Journal of Intelligence and Counterintelligence*, vol. 25, no. 1, Spring 2012, pp. 19–43.

Spielmann, Karl, "Using Enhanced Analytic Techniques for Threat Analysis: A Case Study Illustration," *International Journal of Intelligence and Counterintelligence*, vol. 27, no. 1, Spring 2014, pp. 132–155.

Spielmann, Karl, "I Got Algorithm: Can There Be a Nate Silver in Intelligence?" *International Journal of Intelligence and Counterintelligence*, vol. 29, no. 3, Fall 2016, pp. 525–544.

Tetlock, Philip E., *Expert Political Judgment: How Good Is It? How Can We Know?* Princeton University Press, Princeton, 2005.

Tetlock, Philip E. (with Dan Gardner), *Superforecasting: The Art and Science of Prediction*, Crown Publishers, New York, 2015.

Index

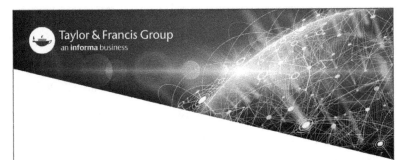